PRAISE FOR
WALKING *in*
BROKEN SHOES

3/23

Insightful quotes, proverbs, and bible verses accompany Sue Walsh's personal account of living and helping through the 2010 earthquake in Haiti. Her personal journey—overcoming her son's tragic death and her injuries from an auto crash, to take on new challenges at work and in service to the neediest children, and leading multiple volunteer medical mission trips—is as inspiring as the unconquerable Haitian spirit she describes.

—SUSAN B. NOYES
Founder of Make It Better

In *Walking in Broken Shoes,* author Susan Walsh has provided a poignant view of the Haiti most of us do not know. Through her experiences as a nurse practitioner in a medical mission, we see Haitians valiantly struggling to meet the most basic of needs—food, water, shelter, health—while retaining hope and a positive attitude. Once you have shared Susan's experiences following the disastrous earthquake of 2010, you will never see Haiti the same way again. The stories in this book will stay with you long after you have replaced it on your bookshelf. My only problem in reading about the many visits of this dedicated medical team to Haiti was the necessity to keep wiping away my tears.

—MARY CAROLE McMANN, MPH
Editor of Nurse Practitioner
World News

Sue Walsh's storytelling and riveting descriptions of her experiences in caring for the health needs of people in Haiti are both chilling and inspiring. I highly recommend *Walking in Broken Shoes* to all as a reminder of how powerful these personal encounters are in making a difference—not only to the people they serve, but also in the lives of care providers.

—AGATHA M. GALLO, PhD, RN, CPNP
Professor, University of Illinois, Chicago
College of Nursing

As the nation's top medical schools incorporate global health programs into their curricula, pediatric nurse practitioner and clinical instructor Susan Walsh similarly integrates her passions for health care, teaching, and service. Leading teams to a mountaintop clinic in Haiti with medical competence and cultural humility, Susan ultimately teaches us all that the most essential element in promoting global health is the human connection. *Walking in Broken Shoes* is an unforgettable read for health care professionals interested in providing meaningful and sustainable care in resource-poor settings.

—LESLIE CORDES, MD, FAAP
Instructor in Pediatrics
Northwestern University
Feinberg School of Medicine

WALKING *in* BROKEN SHOES

A Nurse's Story of Haiti and the Earthquake

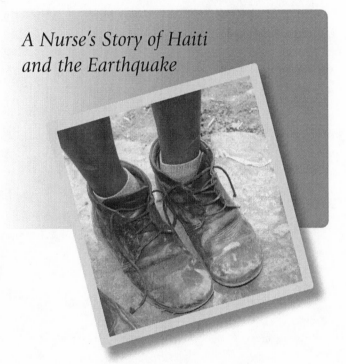

SUSAN MAGNUSON WALSH

LARKSPUR, COLORADO

CULTIVATING JOY

Grace Acres Press
P.O. Box 22
Larkspur, CO 80018
888-700-GRACE (4722)
(303) 681-9995
(303) 681-9996 (fax)
www.GraceAcresPress.com

Grace Acres Press also publishes books in a variety of
electronic formats. Some content that appears in print may
not be available in electronic books.

Library of Congress Cataloging-in-Publication Data:
Walsh, Susan Magnuson.
   Walking in broken shoes : A nurse's story of Haiti and the earthquake /
by Susan Magnuson Walsh.
      p. cm.
   Includes bibliographical references.
   ISBN 978-1-60265-032-9 (pbk.)
1. Walsh, Susan. 2. Haiti Earthquake, Haiti, 2010. 3. Missionaries,
Medical—Haiti. 4. Disaster relief—Haiti. 5. Haiti—Social conditions—
21st century. 6. Haiti—Economic conditions—21st century. I. Title.
   HV600 2010 .H2 W35 2011
      363.34'9558092— dc22
      [B]   2010041539

Printed in the United States of America
13 12 11 10   01 02 03 04 05 06 07 08 09 10

DEDICATED

TO MY TEAMMATES.

TO THE HUNDREDS OF THOUSANDS
OF PEOPLE IN HAITI
WHO LOST THEIR LIVES, A LIMB, A LOVE,
BUT HAVE NOT LOST HOPE.

TO BRAD
WHOSE MEMORY PROVIDES ME
WITH THE UNDERSTANDING OF
EVERLASTING LOVE.

CONTENTS

Be still and know that I am God . . .
—PSALM 46:10

ACKNOWLEDGMENTS

*Every time you cross my mind, I break
out in exclamations of thanks to God.*
—PHILIPPIANS 1:3 (THE MESSAGE)

It is incongruent that an author would lack words, but I am not a professional writer. Therefore, I am not surprised at the inadequacy of my vocabulary to express my thankfulness to all who have supported me and shared my passions. Together we have done many little things in Haiti to decrease suffering, to improve health, and to experience the reciprocity of a very genuine human love for each other. For your continued energy and dedication, which have become contagious, I am grateful. For all who travel to Haiti with me, coordinate supplies, assist with financial gifts, and lift up our teams and Haiti in prayer, you are a blessing.

The depth of my love and gratitude to you, Brian, is completely inexpressible. Your constant support is unwavering and without your humble dedication and deep faith, our service in Haiti would never have developed to fruition.

Maggie and Kyle, you are the joys of my life and I thank you from every corner of my soul for returning my love moment to moment, year after year. It's because of you, my precious children, that I can almost imagine the fullness of joy in God's promises.

I would be remiss if I didn't acknowledge my gratitude to the rest of my family and friends. There is no one in my life who has not succumbed to one of my Haiti stories. Thank you profusely for listening, caring, and always rallying around me when I am in need.

To my editing buddies, please receive this very special and wildly robust word of thanks. You know who you are! You graciously gave clarity and direction to my frequently rambling thoughts. My appreciation to the team at Grace Acres Press for taking a chance—you must have heard my prayers! Lastly, and most sincerely, I thank you, each reader, who will follow my faith journey through my words.

PREFACE

Piti, piti, wazo fe nich li.
"Little by little the bird builds its nest."
—Haitian Proverb

Since the devastating earthquake in Haiti on Tuesday, January 12, 2010, at 4:53 P.M. EST, millions of eyes have seen, ears have heard, and hearts have felt the anguish of the Haitian people on that dreadful day and thereafter. I am just one of those millions. However, I am also one of a much smaller number who were actually present in Haiti on that same day, just 13 miles from the epicenter of the infamous 7.0 Haitian quake that shook and shuddered the world.

I was completely safe. I did not get hurt. I don't have a search-and-rescue story, so my memoirs may not be exceptional or exciting to read. I do, however, have a story that is deeply human in nature, about precious people, survival and hardship, grace and hope, and making a difference little by little.

Before 2010, I had made six trips to Haiti with various medical teams. Many people became interested in our work in Haiti prior to the earthquake. I have had the pleasure of spending time answering questions and exchanging ideas with them. However, many more family, friends, acquaintances, and even complete strangers have become deeply interested since January 12, 2010. Because of this, I am carefully compiling my thoughts here in an effort to honestly and coherently answer the many sincere queries about the earthquake itself, our work in Haiti, Haiti's situation since the quake, and the future for Haiti. I hope to respond to those asking with respect for each and every Haitian, and with a level of detail that will satisfy each inquirer's intellect and heart.

Please be aware that this book contains my interpretations and opinions developed from my experiences during many hours spent in Haiti working, observing, discussing, and feeling. I am not a sociologist, anthropologist, historian, physician, or politician, so I am acutely aware of my limitations. However, I believe myself to be a member of the world's theoretical "society of humanitarians." I have eagerly opened myself to the flow of life, knowing that this flow will continue to mold that which I am and will influence my ever-growing and changing thoughts. I welcome input and the exchange of experiences and opinions from all in hopes of deepening enlightenment.

It can be frustrating to be unable to find the perfect combination of vocabulary and emphasis to adequately share the sights, sounds, smells, physical sensations, and emotions of such a profound and life-changing experience. Even more unnerving over time will be the challenge of personally integrating each memory in a way that retains the detail of a photograph but doesn't cause nightmares, an inability to sleep, eat, laugh, carry on, experience joy, and keep one's faith. As humans we are all thus challenged.

PROLOGUE: PHOTOGRAPHS

Photography is a way of feeling, of touching, of loving. What you have caught on film is captured forever . . . it remembers little things, long after you have forgotten everything.
——AARON SISKIND

Have you ever looked at a photograph intensely, willing the memory to come back, wishing for the absolute moment in time to come vividly alive again? Sometimes staring at a picture returns not only the flood of a particular memory, but also its feeling: of fresh air, grainy sand between toes, cool tide water and clean tap water, freezing snow causing nose drips, dirt in teeth and dust in eyes.

Somehow the sweet aroma of flowers and wet grass startles the senses again, along with lingering scents of warm cookies, turkey, sweat on a little boy's head, sweat on a Haitian man in the field. The remembered sounds that float from a picture can be as true as a daughter playing violin in the next room, cheers at a hockey game, friendly hollers carried by a strong Haitian breeze during an after-school *futball* game, dogs and roosters at dawn that are not even visible in a mountainside photo.

Memories of voices heard and recognized recall the exact content, tone, and quality of words, at that moment . . . when looking at a photograph.

Occasionally there is the disappointment of a photo that won't work its magic. I can see the picture and say, "Oh, yeah, I remember that," but the emotion doesn't come back. During the struggle to feel, hear, or smell the scene, nothing is elicited. In fact, if I didn't see myself in the picture, I wouldn't believe I had ever been in the scene. That doesn't happen too often, but often enough to elicit a green envy wish that I had been more like my scrapbooking friends, who date and document each photo.

My favorite response from a picture is when my gaze locks onto the eyes of someone I love and my heart skips a beat. Like a picture of my husband, Brian, or the precious blue-eyed glances from each of my three children's pictures, or the warmth of deep brown eyes melting my heart like sweet, hot chocolate sauce as I recall, *"Bonjour Madame!"* There can also be a breath-stopping photo that induces so much pain that the picture has to be put out of sight.

Then there are the pictures that are only in the mind . . .

The wisdom of nations lies in their proverbs, which are brief and pithy.
—WILLIAM PENN

PART ONE

BEFORE THE EARTHQUAKE

1 | THE START

Like good stewards of the manifold Grace of God; Serve one another with whatever gift each of you has received.
—1 PETER 4:10

MY HUSBAND, BRIAN, A CARPENTER, AND I, A PEDIATRIC NURSE, LIVED A JOY-FILLED LIFE TOGETHER AS WE RAISED OUR THREE CHILDREN: BRAD, MAGGIE, AND KYLE. THE CHILDREN WERE COMPLETING THEIR SCHOOLING AND BRIAN AND I WERE INVOLVED IN WELL-SUITED CAREERS AND HOBBIES. WE WERE ALL FOLLOWING LIFE PATHS THAT WERE RATHER TYPICAL. OUR THOUGHTS WERE IN THE MOMENT, BUT WE HAD EXCITING VISIONS FOR THE FUTURE. FAMILY AND FRIENDS ENCIRCLED US IN A COMFORTABLE COCOON AND THE CONSTANCY OF OUR FAITH GUIDED OUR DECISIONS.

THEN, ON A FATAL NIGHT IN MAY 2003, OUR HEARTS AND LIVES WERE WRENCHED APART FOREVER AS WE LOST OUR 21-YEAR-OLD SON, BRAD, TO A MOTOR VEHICLE ACCIDENT. JUST A FEW SHORT MONTHS FOLLOWING THE TRAGEDY OF LOSING BRAD, AS I WALKED across the street at a very busy intersection, a car struck me. My leg was broken, both of my knees were injured, and I was required to follow a non-weight-bearing regimen for a three-month recovery period, with physical therapy for six months. There were solace and respite to be found in my recovery, and I discovered both physical and emotional renewal, becoming stronger each day. Near the end of my activity restrictions, I received a surprising phone call. The call was a request to become a clinical instructor for graduate nurses in a pediatric nurse practitioner program in Chicago. The thought of change was appealing. I accepted the position.

As I started teaching pediatric nurses in graduate school, I quickly came to the realization that I would have an influence on adult thinkers. Stepping into the world of academia, I recognized that my 30 years of nursing experience were assets. I knew I would have the opportunity to direct students' medical learning and expansion of their advanced nursing practice. I was, however, uncertain of the guiding role I might play with the students in regard to humanitarian service. I also discovered a new personal compass, directing me toward helping and serving others, especially children of all ages, races, and socioeconomic status—especially those most vulnerable. I was very energized by the prospect of integrating my passions for health, pediatrics, and service. Working with students in a medical mission abroad appeared to be an opportunity for eager minds to join in my pursuits. Could I be so bold as to expose others to and engage them in my ideologies, in the university setting?

I allowed my mind to wander and my conversations to seek out the medical travel experiences of others. I filled my calendar with meetings with anyone who had done medical mission work, querying and exhausting those in my path. I did a robust literature search on the concept of service learning. Recruiting proficient, expert colleagues to join my travels was desirable and would provide a richer experience for the students. I received a qualified approval from my department heads to develop a low-profile proposal. I was rolling forward and ready to accelerate.

After a year of seeking and deliberation, Haiti became our destination of choice. I read a remarkable book, *Mountains beyond Mountains*, by Tracy Kidder, written about Paul Farmer, who is a legend in the international-developing countries-medical-sociological-anthropological-humanitarian world. I also spoke with a dear friend who had just returned from a poor mountain village outside of Port-au-Prince, Haiti, where he had successfully performed simple surgical procedures over the course of a week. He went with a small medical team. They stayed at a missionary's house, and were well fed and exceptionally well cared for. I contacted the missionaries, and they were open to my idea of bringing a medical team focused on pediatrics to their clinic. They had a few medical teams committed to their medical mission vision who came a few times a year, but were excited to have another group interested in serving in their poor village. At that time Haiti had 2 doctors to every 10,000 people, which equates to little or no care for the majority. This seemed like a good destination.

As I sought out information about Haiti, I quickly learned more than I initially wanted to know. Not only was Haiti by far the poorest country in the Western hemisphere, it was one of the poorest and least developed countries in the world. Haiti has struggled with problems ranging from near-constant political upheaval to health crises and food crises, to severe environmental degradation, to the assurance of an annual barrage of hurricanes. I paused for a minute as I assimilated Haiti's history, which is replete with the ravages of poverty.

Haiti occupies an area roughly the size of Maryland on the Caribbean island of Hispaniola; it has 8.7 million residents of African descent who speak Creole and French. Four out of five people live in poverty, and more than half subsist in abject poverty. Deforestation and overfarming have left much of Haiti eroded and barren, vulnerable to mudslides during heavy rain. In the 18th century, the western portion of Hispaniola was one of the richest colonies in the French empire, known for its lucrative sugar-cane and coffee plantations. In 1791, the African slave population revolted, eventually winning independence from Napoleon Bonaparte's

France. Freeing itself from colonial rule, it became the world's first black republic.

The country, renamed Haiti, was required to pay high fees to France as retribution and restitution for land, equipment, and each slave that France had owned. This was the beginning of freedom for Haiti—along with an insurmountable financial burden that Haiti would not reconcile with France until 1947.

Haiti's history has been marked by many periods of profound political disarray, including frequent changes of government, military coups, and (beginning in 1915) a two-decade occupation by the United States.

François Duvalier, called "Papa Doc," became president in 1957, beginning a long rule known for corruption and human rights abuses. His son, Jean-Claude Duvalier, known as "Baby Doc," controlled the country from 1971 until he fled in 1986, during an upheaval that led to another period of alternating civilian and military rule. In 1991, Jean-Bertrand Aristide took power, but was overthrown shortly after taking office by a violent coup that initiated a three-year period of military rule. The military's government ended only after the intervention of a United Nations force led by the United States.

The 1995 election of René Préval, a prominent political ally of Mr. Aristide, was widely praised, but subsequent elections—including Mr. Aristide's restoration to his old post in 2000—were plagued by allegations of fraud. In February 2004, after groups opposed to the Aristide government seized control of cities and towns throughout Haiti, Mr. Aristide resigned and fled to South Africa. U.S.-led armed forces were sent to Port-au-Prince to stabilize the situation and to oversee the installation of an interim government.

The United Nations has spent some $5 billion on peacekeeping operations since 2004. In the first part of 2005, there was talk of Mr. Préval again being considered for election for president, amidst allegations of impropriety, with the national election scheduled for fall of 2005.

Haiti's history is astounding, and in 2005 the country was quite unstable politically, economically, and socially. A significant lack of infrastructure impaired all arenas of life. At the root of this crisis was the persistence of an ineffective government, along with poorly controlled eruptions of social violence that required UN occupation. Haiti appeared to lack an effective policing and judicial system. Corruption was the norm. The government failed to consistently influence education or health care, and nongovernmental organizations (NGOs) were a significant factor in what stability was achieved among the people. Haiti is a country of many religious affiliations; in particular, the centuries-long influence of voodoo affects Haitian culture and the practice of medicine. Integrating Haitian patients' cultural beliefs, which are their truths, with a desire for conventional medical treatments, which they also know to be effective, is a challenge and a difficult balance.

The U.S. State Department has persistently had a travel advisory warning for the uneducated traveler. In 2005, Haiti was definitely not the vacation spot in the Caribbean that it used to be. However, I concluded that the need in Haiti was great, and that a small effort on my (our) part could be significant, even if for just a few. I wanted to take my students to a place where they had never been, on both a physical and an emotional plane: A place of unignorable influence that would form them, where resources were limited, and where they would have to think out of the traditional health-care-system box. A place where the ravages of poverty and poor health care would present disease states not seen in America. I was seeking a situation where they would have a deep humanitarian experience that would change them forever, molding their careers in a way that I could never teach in the classroom. My students were immediately engaged by this opportunity. Graduate students are willing, adventurous, intelligent, capable, and flexible, all of which are perfect attributes for traveling companions.

I can't say that I was surprised at a few of the initial reactions to my idea, but I was surprised that the negative and offensive reactions were the majority. Comments ranged from "Sue, are you crazy?" to "Susie, you are likely seeking something to fill the ache in your heart after losing Brad, which is probably a good, healing thing [respectful pause] . . . but why don't you find something less dangerous to do to get your mind off your tragic loss?" to "Susan, the university's legal department isn't supportive of your travel plans to Haiti."

I have a pretty good self-awareness, but my husband, Brian, knows me even better than I know myself, and he absolutely realizes how all that I do plays out in our lives. He is completely aware of my faith, and of my dedication first to my family, then to my friends, then to my career and all that it stands for. He understands that I have always wanted to be an unconventional missionary of sorts. He knows that after we lost Brad we both developed a new perspective on life and time, and that an appreciation for both beyond comprehension became our aura. He knew that all of these things were why I wanted to go to Haiti, and he understood. His response was the one I cared most about: "Mags [his nickname for me], if you want to do this, I will come with you!"

2 | February 2006: Act

Neg di san fe.
"People talk and don't act."
—Haitian Proverb

For the rest of the year 2005, I became a master seeker and organizer: seeker of knowledge about tropical diseases, Haitian culture, French Creole, and voodoo; organizer of medication and supplies to bring to Haiti, students and other willing trippers, paperwork, waivers, airline tickets, and funding. I dug deeper into Haitian current events to fully grasp the impact the impending 2005 election would have on our plans.

The 2004 Haitian rebellion resulted in a coup d'état, in which Jean-Bertrand Aristide was removed from office and exiled from Haiti via a U.S. plane accompanied by U.S. military/security personnel. I had heard about that at the time, but hadn't paid too much attention, and hadn't realized that controversy remained regarding the extent of U.S. involvement in Aristide's departure and whether or not the departure was voluntary. I learned that a "council of the wise" had been set up by the international powers to choose a new prime minister, but that this procedure was not in accordance with the Haitian constitution. This interim government of the council, led by Prime Minister Gerard Latortue (brought back from the United States) and President Boniface Alexandre, was installed in Haiti on March 12, 2004. Even with my limited previous knowledge of non-mainstream international politics, I could recognize that this political maneuver wasn't stellar. I could see why the political analysts were anticipating a level of dissension among the people, considering Haiti's 200-year history of unsettled, inefficient, corrupt democracy and multiple violent political eruptions. With deliberate consideration and a healthy respect for whatever negative events might develop, we decided to travel to Haiti in early 2006, which seemed to be a very reasonable time span between the scheduled presidential election in October 2005 and our planned departure date of February 22, 2006. We felt that we were being very logical, prudent, and responsible in allowing several months between the two dates.

Unfortunately, the 2005 elections to replace Haiti's interim government were delayed four times, after having been scheduled originally for October and November 2005. Of course, there were many reasons for the Haitian election delays. The voter registration deadline, set for early August, was not met because of lack of funding. There was considerable unrest in the slums of Port-au-Prince, attacks were made on the existing "council," and the UN and the Haitian National Police were accused of committing massacres and targeted killings of anti-occupation protesters and organizers. However, the inability to register voters in the time allocated, along with the plan to place only 800 to 900 voting stations throughout Haiti (in contrast to the several thousands established in previous elections), were both very troubling situations. Also, the new plan to have no voting stations in Cité

Soleil, an extremely impoverished and heavily populated area where makeshift armies professed allegiance to Aristide, would require these registered voters to leave their neighborhood to vote. Traveling outside of this slum area would cause a hardship most residents of Cité Soleil could not overcome, and therefore 300,000 to 600,000 people would realistically have no vote.

With each postponement, I learned more about Haitian governmental policies—or lack thereof—and I began to understand the huge disparities between the government and the people. It also was hard to miss the forward march of the calendar, daily reducing the distance between our already-paid-for departure and the date for the elections. From the inception of this trip, I was faithfully and constantly praying for direction and guidance, for wisdom and leadership. Now I was literally praying fervently for peace for a country I barely knew but for which I felt a newfound fondness definitely developing.

The first round of elections finally took place on February 7, 2006, only two weeks prior to our date of departure. At that time our airline carrier announced closure of all flights going to Haiti, as the U.S. State Department had listed Haiti as a "no travel" destination with a strong enough advisory that commercial flights were unswervingly heeding the warnings. According to official statistics, René Préval led the count for president with 48.8 percent of the vote. However, this was less than the 50 percent required for him to be declared elected on the first round of voting, even though Préval's initial vote count was more than 60 percent of the total. Election officials of the interim government ordered a halt to the publication of full election results pending an inquiry into possible electoral fraud. Declarations of invalid votes, and allegations of fraud, errors, and the discovery of perhaps thousands of ballots dumped and burned in Port-au-Prince, marred the authenticity of this election, like so many other elections over the centuries.

As the electoral council announced that Préval's vote count had slipped below the 50 percent required to avoid a second round of voting, thousands of his supporters marched through Port-au-Prince in protest at what they claimed was an effort to manipulate the vote count and suppress support for Préval. Of the 2.2 million ballots cast, roughly 125,000 were declared invalid. A further 4 percent of the ballots were blank but were nonetheless added to the count, thereby lowering the percentage of the vote per candidate. Finally, on February 16, following days of protests by Préval supporters, and meetings between the electoral council and the interim government, it was agreed that blank ballots would be distributed among the candidates. Blank ballots were counted as abstentions. All of this eventually resulted in a total vote for Préval of 51.1 percent. A second round of voting for president was thus avoided.

This ballot business was reminiscent of the Bush–Gore 2000 ballot debacle, but in America violence never loomed. My own investment in our presidential election process was minimal compared to my personal and financial investment made to this Haitian stew that was considerably stirred up. I was attempting to wrap my mind around all the potentially adverse event scenarios, should we actually travel to Haiti at this time. I decided that if no violence was evident, and the airlines opened their flights, the choice of going as a team to Haiti would be put out for discussion. Granted, there were a lot of "ifs," but I felt that the value of our trip was still worthy of an educated debate. As providential timing would have it, our scheduled flight was the first that the airlines reopened. A dozen of us felt God directing the forward movement of our trip. We packed 24 suitcases full of supplies, we put our personal belongings in small carry-ons, we started our malaria prophylaxis, and we boarded the plane.

EMAIL: FEBRUARY 2006

12 of us took our first trip to Haiti, arriving in Port-au-Prince one week after the elections for a new president. The elections were postponed several times from the fall of 2005 to Feb. 2006. When they were finally held, Préval was elected. Political unrest was expected, so flights into [Port-au-Prince]

PAP were canceled and our flights to Miami were waylaid. There was little to no rioting and we eventually made it into PAP with no difficulties. Willem, the founder of the clinic, school, and church, a missionary and our host, met us at the airport. Our first experience through customs was stressful but successful, and we made it to the village by mid-morning. We went directly to the clinic and unpacked, stocked the pharmacy, and set up our exam stations. Villagers were forming lines and we were eager to start clinic. We saw over 1,000 people in desperate need of medical care. We treated many severe skin and scalp infections and multiple respiratory infections such as pneumonia, bronchitis, and asthma. Many children also had ear, eye, and sinus infections. We treated all the school children and almost every village child who came to the clinic with de-worming medication, also providing vitamins to each child and to all the lactating mothers. The children who were severely malnourished were also given peanut butter. Many infants and children had other gastrointestinal problems, and we were able to provide medications, re-hydrating solutions, and intravenous [fluids] to those in need. Our pharmaceutical supplies never ran out!

It quickly spread through the mountains that "Le blanc ici" (literally meaning "the white here"). There had been no medical team there since September 2005. News traveled fast, and we were faced with crowds of typically 200 patients per day, some traveling for 3 days, over 2 mountains, to get to the clinic. We started at 5:00 A.M., organizing ourselves, doing a devotion, eating breakfast, and then traveling several miles in the back of an old pickup truck, over rocky, steep mountain "roads" to the clinic. We ended our patient day as the sun went down, around 6:30, sometimes finishing by flashlight, since there is no electricity in the clinic. Some families actually waited all day to be seen, never complaining, and always appreciative. As we returned to the missionary's home where we stayed, we had a nice dinner waiting for us. We then took a quick "Haitian bath" (which consists of a bin of water and a pitcher), reviewed important clinical information, and found it important to fellowship and share with one another. Bed wasn't far off, and soon the roosters and the dogs were waking us up for another day. On Sunday we took the day off and worshiped with the villagers in their beautiful handmade church.

Each day was a new and overwhelming experience, and we felt God's guidance and presence in everything we did. Willem, born and raised in Haiti, along with his wife Beth and two young children, Stephan and David, were kind and graceful hosts. Willem, whose family history goes back to the slave revolution, was willing to share with us a lot about himself and about Haiti, talking with us late into the night. He is fascinating, with an impressive vision for his missionary work and for his country.

Thanks to Willem and his family, our brief mission was safely accomplished. It was hard to leave, since we knew there were so many more children to care for. We sadly looked into the binoculars toward the clinic as we were leaving for the airport, and saw yet another line forming. Tears came along with the promise of a return visit.

Brian and Sue

3 | JANUARY 2007: HELP

At the same time, the fact the world's poor are calling upon us to help is a marker, in my view, of the limitless potential of human solidarity.
—PAUL FARMER

I HAD A FLOOD OF EMOTIONS AND IDEAS AS I CONTEMPLATED THE KALEIDOSCOPE OF IMAGES AND EXPERIENCES AFTER OUR FIRST TRIP.

WHAT IS NEEDED TO SUSTAIN OUR MISSION WORK IN HAITI? AS I TRY TO PROCESS THIS QUESTION, AN UNCOMFORTABLE FEELING OVERTAKES ME. I HAVE BEEN TRYING, EVER SINCE MY FIRST TRIP TO HAITI, TO DEFINE THAT AWKWARD, UNSETTLING EMOTION. RECOGNITION HAS FINALLY SETTLED UPON ME: I'M NOT SURE I KNOW WHAT IS NEEDED. I'M NOT QUALIFIED TO SAY. AS I LIE IN MY VERY COMFY BED AFTER A NICE SHOWER AND A FULL APPLICATION OF FRAGRANT LOTIONS, MY WINDOWS OPEN WITH A SOFT, FRESH BREEZE FILTERING IN, I'M UNABLE TO SETTLE DOWN AND RELAX BECAUSE I HAVE A FEW ITCHY BUG BITES ON MY ANKLES AND arms. I think of the Haitian children I know, sleeping on concrete beds or on the floor, straw under a worn blanket to soften the concrete, no shower, no screens, who are scratching their scabies and other infestations night after night, to the point of severe infection, distraction, and discomfort. I want to buy enough medication and soap to rid them of these infestations and infections. Effective medication is expensive, but it's strong and it works. And this suffering is relieved, even if it is only for a few months.

EMAIL: JANUARY 2007

Our team of 16 volunteers took our second medical mission trip to Haiti, where we go to a small mountain village about an hour away from Port-au-Prince, the capital of Haiti. The clinic where we work is in the middle of a very steep and rocky mountain, in a very poor village, where people have very small, concrete houses, no running water or plumbing (no toilets or showers), no electricity, no appliances, no roads, no cars, no stores . . . they eat what they can grow amidst the rocks. They have very little livestock, only a few chickens or goats; a few have a pig. They cook on an open fire outside.

The villagers have to walk to the middle of the mountain where a cistern has been built to collect water from a fresh spring at the top of the mountain which then comes down the mountain and out of a spigot, where they fill their buckets with water, then carry the full water buckets on their heads back to their homes, miles away, to use for drinking, cooking, washing, and watering their fields. Phew—it is a very difficult life. The missionaries with whom we stay have built a church, school, and health clinic by the water spigot, so the children can go to school during the day, and bring water home after school. For the children who live too far [away] to travel every day, there are no public schools, and no clean water.

The reason we go to this village is to provide health care to pregnant women, infants, children, and their families, who would otherwise have no health care at all. There are no vaccines, no preventative medicine, and no treatment for anyone when they are sick. They are far away from the city of Port-au-Prince, and there is no form of transportation for them and no money to pay for health care, even if they could get to the city.

They suffer from many kinds of diseases, infections, fungus, skin infestations, intestinal worms and malnutrition—mostly from the intestinal worms, which consume all of the nutrition from whatever food they eat. Since they have very little eggs, milk, or meat, they are also anemic, which affects their energy level and ability to concentrate. They are very uncomfortable, and it is extremely sad to witness this level of suffering which is so easily treatable. The fortunate children, who live close enough to attend the school, receive lunch consisting of rice and beans during the school week, which may be the only meal they have for the day. They receive vitamins regularly and de-worming medication when available, all [of] which helps tremendously to keep them much healthier.

During the time we are there, we are able to see and treat over 200 people daily. We provide them with medications for infections, infestations, worms, and for illnesses we can safely treat; we give each child, lactating and pregnant women vitamins, and we give peanut butter to children who are extremely malnourished—peanut butter is perfect since it is high in protein, high in fat, does not need refrigeration, and tastes great! We also try to provide soap and toothbrushes to as many as we can.

So why do we go to a country which is so far away and on the State Department's travel advisory list? That's a hard question to answer. We believe that God depends on us to do His work. We are His hands and feet. He always tries to tell us what He wants us to do, if we take the time to be still and listen. He gives us a heart for doing something special. We all know that each of us has special gifts, and we glorify God if we use those gifts in ways to help others. It has taken me a lot of years caring for sick children in this country in order to have the confidence and courage to go into a strange country, with unusual diseases and conditions, but God put the situation in front of me, and I listened. I felt it in my heart that I could do this. I just needed to find others who also felt they could serve in this way. I trusted God. Over the year that I decided to try to put together a medical mission team, 11 other people came to me, and we organized our first team. Lots of kids, parents, friends, and parishioners heard about our *dreams to bring medical care, medication, vitamins, and peanut butter to Haiti, and they joined in to help. God has been certain to provide us with what we have needed, with safe travels, and with lots of support from people of all ages, with all kinds of gifts to offer up in service. Children, good health, and doing something exciting and adventurous are all my passions, so I guess God knows me pretty well and has given me the opportunity to really enjoy serving Him.*

Sue Walsh

4 | JANUARY 2008: BALANCE

> *Bondye do ou: fe pa ou, M a fe pa M.*
> *"God says do your part and I'll do mine."*
> —HAITIAN PROVERB

UPON RETURNING FROM OUR SECOND TRIP, I REAL-IZED SOMETHING SIGNIFICANT WAS MISSING. I ABSOLUTELY KNEW THAT I WOULD NEVER BE CUL-TURALLY ASSIMILATED, CULTURALLY COMPETENT, OR HAVE THE OPPORTUNITY FOR FULL IMMERSION IN HAITI. HOWEVER, I REFUSED TO HAVE A LEVEL OF IGNORANCE ABOUT OUR WORK RELATING TO A CUL-TURAL FRAMEWORK. I HAD READ MUCH OF PAUL FARMER'S WORK AND ATTENDED ONE OF HIS INFOR-MATIVE LECTURES, LEARNING MORE ABOUT THE ORGANIZATION HE FOUNDED, PARTNERS IN HEALTH, AND HIS WORK WITH THE WORLD HEALTH ORGANI-ZATION. I WANTED TO INTEGRATE THE IMPORTANCE OF PARTNERING WITH HAITIANS, TO TAKE THEIR LEAD AND SUPPORT THEIR DESCRIBED NEEDS IN ALL WE PLANNED TO DO. I WAS DETERMINED NOT TO become a clinical or even altruistic tourist. The importance of sustainability, ensuring continuity of care within an existing system, attention to safety, and environmental considerations, along with a sense of shared responsibility, became paramount. I was adopting the concept of *cultural humility*, first elaborated in 1998 by Tervalon and Murray-Garcia. Their theory acknowledges that not only is the acquisition of cultural competency—when an outsider develops a thorough knowledge of the beliefs and norms of another culture—extremely difficult, but also that being sensitive to another's culture is not enough. Cultural humility requires us to take responsibility for our interactions with others beyond sensitivity, to approach others as equals in spite of differences in beliefs or behaviors and to have complete respect for others' beliefs and cultural norms.

The influence of voodoo has affected Haitian culture for centuries. The majority of Haitians do not regularly practice voodoo, but they do fear the potential negative effects of bad voodoo. I have observed that our Haitian patients frequently see the effects or outcomes of voodoo practice as explanations for the inexplicable, a divergence of a conceptual reference point. The most common situations lacking explanation, where Western medicine and Haitian perceptions split, are with regard to mental and unobservable physical ailments. For example, if an individual is demonstrating an abnormal behavior pattern of extreme and continued sadness, Western culture might diagnose that individual with depression and treat him or her with psychiatric care and medication. In Haitian culture, the diagnosis would likely be that "the person caught the voodoo," in which case others would likely stay away from that individual for fear of the voodoo leaving the suffering person and jumping onto the healthy individual. Other common beliefs are that one can catch the voodoo through a bad spirit traveling within the wind, lingering at the threshold of the home, or spreading through contagious contact.

I have experienced the challenge of balancing Western medicine with Haitian culture many times in the clinic, while striving to integrate cultural humility, maintaining a high standard of medical care, and integrating concepts learned from Paul Farmer. I can set goals for myself and my team as I assimilate what I've experienced in the village with what is apparent to me with my pediatric and maternal focus and my heart for compassion. I can try hard to do my part, and to encourage others to do their part, and we will have to leave the rest to God.

EMAIL: JANUARY 2008— HI FROM HAITI!

Our team of 18 made it through our travels safely and has arrived at the village! We had an angel at the airport who arranged our bag tags and "heavy tags" for our luggage, so we paid no fines for several bags which were definitely over 50 lbs and she allowed us to bring 3 extra bags. Our plane was delayed leaving Miami, so we arrived in Port-au-Prince late and had to travel through the city and into the mountains in the dark. We did not have our usual UN escort, which made the journey a little scary and possibly unpredictable, but that's when we felt the presence of your prayers the most—which was a great way to start our mission.

As was typical, we woke to the roosters and dogs at sunrise and the first thing I did was look through the binoculars to see the people already lined up at the clinic, walking from every direction to the center of the mountain where the clinic is located. We've had 3 productive clinic days so far, seeing so many in need, with bad infections, skin infestations, worms, and more. The good news is that there have also been many healthy pregnant and nursing moms, healthy babies, and returning patients coming back to the clinic for refills of their medications! Also, we have with us a wonderful Haitian nurse, who is helping us in so many ways. It would be great if she can continue in the clinic between medical teams!

Tomorrow we are going to church, to 2 orphanages to care for the children and then back to clinic Monday and Tuesday. We've had a few heartbreaks, with children being very sick, but also saw some amazing elderly couples, and our good friend, the 77-year-old village midwife and his wife—who asked us if we might have just a little rubbing alcohol we might spare to use for his deliveries (and he was very happy with his new cowboy hat!).

*We had enough money to purchase everything we needed, and to provide
vitamins and peanut butter to all, including the 600 schoolchildren here in
the village, for the next 6 months. Thank you again for your thoughts and
prayers, keep it up—we won't be home until Wednesday!*

Brian and Sue

EMAIL: JANUARY 2008— HI FROM GLENVIEW!

*We made it home safely last night, grateful for the country of abundance
we live in, but sad to leave our friends in Haiti who are still in so much
need. Again we were able to see well over a thousand people in our short
clinic week, along with providing everything the 600 school children might
need for the next six months. We also were able to see and treat the children and provide access to medications and vitamins to two orphanages in
Port-au-Prince. Brian and David actually had the privilege to help prepare
a new home for the orphans with their carpentry work, and to move their
belongings into their new home during the week. The reconstructed beds and
new shelves were very much appreciated!*

*Another new experience for us this year was to go into the mountains
of the village to treat a few people who were too sick to travel down to the
clinic. One woman was in congestive heart failure and certainly would not
have survived beyond a few more days had we not intervened. Not only
were we able to turn around her condition, we also were able to teach our
new Haitian nurse, Euclid, how to continue to evaluate her symptoms and
provide the necessary medications, nutrition, and nursing advice to keep
her stable. Euclid will also be able to do the same for many other villagers
we saw who were unable to travel. We all gained such honor and respect for
each villager as we climbed just a short way into the mountains, with our
healthy bodies, nice shoes, comfortable backpacks, and fresh water bottles.
We saw many patients who walked over one or two mountains, taking a
few days, either being sick themselves or carrying their sick child/children,
sleeping outside in the cold mountain air. It's really unimaginable!*

Many of the children were sicker than we've ever seen before, with very bad infections and conditions such as kwashiorkor. We had "extra cash" that we were able to use to provide extended care for these children in a hospital in Port-au-Prince. God definitely brought to us those very much in need! But ironically we also saw that the schoolchildren were healthier than ever, and we saw many very healthy pregnant women and young infants—all were breast-feeding. We also had the unexpected pleasure of having several people who were so old they actually didn't know their age, accompanied by grandchildren or great-grandchildren, find their way to the clinic. Many were blind from cataracts, but otherwise were in surprisingly good health (no teeth). We provided them with vitamins, arthritis pain medication, eyedrops, medication for acid reflux, sunglasses, hats, and gained so much pleasure from seeing such happy, healthy Haitians, who have worked such a hard life—we all were about to burst! You were all definitely there with us, helping us with thought and prayer.

Now we're back home, many of us off to work today, in our comfortable, clean, and well-stocked clinics, health care access all around us, seeing the inequity of life, but thanking God for the opportunity to balance things out just a bit, little by little.

God bless all of you!
Brian and Sue

5 | June 2008: See

Our drivers in Haiti have all been very experienced in maneuvering all kinds of vehicles on all types of terrain, whether in the mountains, or through the narrow and irregular passages and the mayhem of the city streets. Very few traffic rules are observed in the areas of Haiti that Brian and I have traveled, which over the years has been throughout Port-au-Prince, in and out of many surrounding urban areas, and up and down into the mountains. The one rule of the road I've noted to be consistent everywhere is that if a driver is making a move, either to pass a slower or stalled vehicle or to travel through an intersection, the driver's move must be made with considerable speed and with the horn blaring. Other than that, the roads are open game, and the drivers we have ridden with scale the rocky, uneven, broken-down pavement with amazing skill and finesse.

The drivers have no problem avoiding moving or abandoned vehicles of all shapes and sizes and in various states and conditions. "Taptaps" are a particular nuisance and are in abundance on the road. Picture an old pickup truck with skinny wood benches built into each side of the bed of the truck, with sides and a top for the bed constructed out of whatever materials are available, either metal or wood. Imagine a vivid palette of color splashed on every inch of the truck in exquisite designs, with an overlay of a Scripture verse or an exclamation in either Creole or English such as "Mon Amie Jesus"or "Thank You Lord Everybody" or "Sexy Girl!" Inside the bed of the truck, crammed on the two benches, will be 20 or 30 passengers; some riders will be hanging off the back of the bed or standing on the runners on the sides of the truck. When a passenger desires to terminate a ride, he or she taps repeatedly on the roof or side of the moving vehicle, loud enough for the driver to recognize the sound and stop the truck just long enough for the rider to jump down into the street. Taptaps are consistently amusing to observe, and a ride I would like to take at some juncture in my life.

Old or crashed, inoperable vehicles, of all makes and models, are regularly abandoned in the streets at the exact location of their breakdown, left to be stripped of any material or item that could possibly be used for whatever, by whomever discovers the treasure first. You can spot skeletal vehicles on every road you travel, city or mountain. Willem explained that when a car or truck breaks down due to a mechanical issue or an accident causing extreme disrepair, if the owner has no mechanical skill or monetary resources, the vehicles are just left where they died, on the side of the road or even jutting out into the road. Some owners will strip and sell viable engine parts, use-able pieces of the interior, and metal from the body for scrap. Others will just walk away. Many lone vehicles are used as residences, where people store their belongings and develop a strategy for sleeping in such a street location. Most of the other skeletons naturally become garbage receptacles and pig pens for several adult swine and possibly a young litter.

Besides the taptaps and the abandoned vehicles, motor scooters whiz by in every direction with anywhere from two to four passengers balanced on the seat. The driver must develop 360-degree radial vision to prevent collisions. Pedestrians, who are in great numbers and are everywhere, walk up and down the road, crossing over the road randomly, whenever and wherever it suits them. More often than not, women walk rapidly, with an upright posture and a fluid grace, while balancing a large bucket of water or an oversized basket filled with fruits, vegetables, or other heavy supplies, on their heads. Men also walk swiftly, with intention and might, while carrying full bundles of leeks or large twigs, heavy materials, or even a whole slaughtered pig across their shoulders and backs. Children also mill in and out of traffic, either carrying an only slightly smaller version of an adult load, or walking to school in tattered but always well-laundered and colorful uniforms. Children not in school are entrepreneurial, selling wares or trying to wash the windshield of a car or truck stopped in traffic. Many men, women, and children wear ill-fitting shoes, flip-flops, or are barefooted. The dexterity and strength of these men and women surpass those of the nimblest mountain goat and strongest oxen.

Initially, our rides to and from the airport were hard-core culture shock. The bombardment of so many variants of sight, sound, smell, and sensation, both pleasant and offensive, would cause sensory overload. The array of beautifully colored and skillfully painted canvas displayed on walls and fences was a spectacular art gallery. My neck would strain as I twisted to look longer at the intricate ironwork and carefully crafted woodcarvings strategically balanced on furniture, developing a fantastic curb appeal. Every day merchants set up their designated spots on the sidewalks, selling wares of all kinds. Fresh fruits, melons, vegetables, and coffee, grown on the small farms in the surrounding mountain villages, are fanned out on blankets on the sidewalks, with side stacks of rolls and bags of beans and coffee.

These, along with rice, are the staples of the city dweller's diet, if they can afford to pay. Vendors sell a more limited variety of meats, mostly chicken and goat, which are usually precooked and ready to eat. Clothing, with many recognizable logos, is in piles on the sidewalk or hanging from rope or anything else that will support a hanger or can act as a hook, in order to show off the garments. Shoes are also strewn about and available for purchase.

Many other items are also randomly for sale on the sidewalks, such as tires, mattresses, furniture, and an occasional appliance. Street vending seems to be the accepted use of the sidewalks and curbs. The store owners and residents in the buildings behind the street vendors seem to pay no attention to the merchants' set-ups or the regular sales that occur in front of their businesses or personal dwellings. The coexistence on the streets is an amazing phenomenon definitely not equaled or tolerated anywhere in the United States.

While passing through the urban areas of Port-au-Prince, we saw large hotels and stately, impressive buildings such as the palace and the cathedral. However, what intrigued me even more were the smaller business buildings and private houses. I would strain to see inside the dim or unlit units, struggling to piece together an impression of a way of life, as I attempted to gain a level of understanding while trying not to judge or rely on preconceptions. My most frequent observations have been of creativity and ingenuity. For example, all personal dwellings have a surrounding wall or gate. I can see how these barriers would be necessary to prevent persistent encroachment and to provide a small semblance of privacy. Unsurprisingly, it is common to see, secured along the top of the walls, heavily coiled barbed wire about a foot high, spanning the entire perimeter of the house. I can imagine that barbed wire is expensive, scarce, and fairly unattractive. What tops the walls as frequently as barbed wire, but is an astute and clever use of natural resources, is a concrete shelf formed along the length of the wall. Embedded densely and randomly in the concrete are long, pointy shards of glass, protruding up at various heights, sharp and menacing, paralleling the same utilitarian function of the barbed wire, while simultaneously casting an interesting allure of color and sparkle. My other favorites showcasing ingenuity are the armchairs made from stacks of old tires. Tied together and cut into a form to support any body position desired, I suppose that these recliners are comfy; add a blanket thrown over as a slipcover, and they become perfect.

There are all kinds of people traveling up and down the sidewalks. The majority are individuals, with an occasional parent holding a child's hand or a grouping of a few. Most seem to move with purpose, but others meander at a leisurely pace, evoking the image of pedestrians along Chicago's Magnificent Mile.

EMAIL: JUNE 2, 2008

Hi everyone—

We made it safely to Haiti, and just wanted you all to know, since many of you have been thinking about us, and praying for our team. Our bags (all 24 of them from Chicago) did not make it to Haiti with us . . . long story with a convoluted saga about them possibly being on their way to Russia. . . . Brian, Willem, Mary, Laura, and Amy learned a new kind of patience waiting in the airport hour after hour, flight after flight . . . finally the last airplane that came into Port-au-Prince, and the last on the conveyor belt, well after dark, had all the bags with our precious cargo!!!!

We have had a lot of rain, which has prevented us from using the trucks up and down the mountain—very, very slippery, which would be unsafe for the trucks . . . up high and steep. So we have walked back and forth to the clinic—a challenge for many—but we all saw so many people waiting in the rain, having walked much farther than we, with ailments and carrying sick children . . . no one questioned what we had to do. Because our day had to end before we were able to care for everyone, many slept outside of the clinic in the mud and rain. . . . Please pray for all of these people. We are off to clinic this morning, and it is not raining yet, in fact, I think I might see a shadow!!! :) The rain, wetness, and slippery rocks and mud just don't seem to bother Haitians. They are so patient, gracious, lovely, strong . . . we are in awe and are learning so much!!!! I will send more later. Many thanks for your thoughts and prayers (please continue).

Brian and Sue

EMAIL: JUNE 9, 2008

Hi again—

We've had a wonderful week of clinic!!! In spite of the difficult weather conditions, God has brought to us many who have been in need for some time. Many women and children, babies, and healthy pregnant women have also made their way. In spite of the rain and clouds, the smiles and hugs from the beautiful people here have brightened our days and we don't even miss the sun!!! As you may know from previous pictures you've seen, people get very dressed up to come to the clinic, wearing their best clothes—out of their respect for us . . . which in this weather is not very practical . . . . However, yesterday a little toddler was completely enchanting as she toddled around the clinic with smiling eyes and wearing fancy white party dress and party shoes, twirling around and tap-tapping her way into our hearts forever. :) What a joy this experience always is for us! We've had enough medications, vitamins, and peanut butter for everyone!!! It's been such a blessing. Thank you to so many!!!

One team member, Jill, who had been studying Haitian history and culture, including voodoo, specifically to share with us and help our under-standing, made an interesting observation: She noticed that in spite of all the hunger, strife, and malcontent that has been in the media about Haiti in the past 6 weeks and has been part of Haitian history for the past 200 years, here in the mountains there is a recognition of peace in the villager's expressions, even when they are not engaging in eye contact—just as they walk, work, or wait. She did not see that in other cities as we drove from Port-au-Prince towards the mountains. These people have so little, but yet they are content. . . . We are all trying to wrap our thoughts around that and to adopt that same attitude—when we are completely honest and open with ourselves, it's not as hard as you might think. :) We'll be worshipping with the village in their church this morning, which is always very moving. We're hoping to get to the orphanage this afternoon. We leave, reluctantly, tomorrow morning.

Thanks again for holding us close in thought and prayer this week.

Brian and Sue

6 | JANUARY 2009: MELISSA

> *Woch nan dio pa konnen doule woch nan soley.*
> *"The rock in the water does not know the pain*
> *of the rock in the sun."*
> —HAITIAN PROVERB

WATER IS MOSTLY A BLESSING, AND ONLY OCCASIONALLY A CURSE. WE TAKE FOR GRANTED OUR STATE OF NORMAL HYDRATION. WHEN WE ARE HEALTHY, WE DON'T HAVE TO WORK VERY HARD AT STAYING HYDRATED. OUR BODIES HAVE HOMEOSTATIC SIGNALS, SUCH AS THIRST AND SWEAT, PLUS A COOL BREEZE WHICH TOGETHER MODERATE THE BODY'S THERMOSTAT AND HYDRATION. IF WE DRINK TOO MUCH WATER, OR DON'T HAVE ACCESS TO WATER, OUR BODIES HAVE THE BEAUTY AND COMPLEXITY OF THE KIDNEY'S COMPLICATED FEEDBACK SYSTEM FOR FLUID REGULATION; ESSENTIALLY, THE SYSTEM DIRECTS US TO PEE OR NOT TO PEE. GENERALLY, BY BEING NEAR WATER, LIFE IS QUITE BALANCED.

I FEEL LIKE A ROCK IN WATER: COOLED AND REFRESHED. I HAVE NEVER PERSONALLY EXPERIENCED life only in the sun, without the essential of water. I have been in a few situations with too much water—my basement has flooded. We cleaned it up. I was in a hurricane during my honeymoon on the small island of St. Thomas: The electricity was off throughout the island for three days. We had no running water in our private honeymoon hut, but the abundance of rain still served a personal, positive purpose. We collected the rainwater in our garbage can and used it to stimulate enough pressure to flush the toilet. Also, as we ran out to collect the water in the garbage can, we were refreshed. We collected the water in a glass and had a drink. When the rains stopped after a week, we dried out. But, of course, I've never been a rock in the sun with no shade or relief. I imagine feeling painfully parched without any spf 70 sunscreen, a hat and polarized sunglasses, were I a rock in the sun.

I am acutely aware of the poverty and malnutrition that are occurring in the mountains we visit in Haiti. It is hard for families to grow food. The soil is rocky; the trees have been razed for fuel. Water is a resource that is difficult to collect and redirect. When we provide vitamins and peanut butter (*medika mamba*), this small gesture can be very significant. Especially for pregnant and lactating moms, and children whose brains are developing and whose minds are open for learning, the protein and fat in peanut butter or in a fortified peanut butter paste is relieving. Children's attention in school is better if they are not suffering from hunger and malnutrition.

I think it's hard to imagine or "know" another person's pain, especially when our worlds are so different. I live in a world of abundance, of life-giving water. I don't know the pain of a rock in the sun, but I am willing to try to learn and do something to help create a little oasis.

EMAIL: JANUARY 9, 2009

Hi everyone!

We arrived safely in Haiti 2 days ago—thank you all for your prayers for traveling mercies! As is typical, we had no Internet for several days and a few luggage glitches, but considering we carried over 1 ton of supplies—lit-

erally (40 suitcases, each with 50 lbs + our carry-ons = > 1 ton)—things went pretty smoothly, with all medications and supplies eventually finding their way to Port-au-Prince. The weather is lovely, the people are welcoming, and there are no political issues here . . . wouldn't you all rather be in Haiti right now?!?

We've had 2 full days of clinic, with lines forming before the roosters and dogs have awakened. We have not yet been able to see everyone before nightfall, but we have been able to see all babies, sick children, elderly, and those traveling from very far away before we leave for the day. The others wait overnight and are happy to be seen sometime the following morning. It gets chilly in the mountains at night and they huddle together (perfect strangers) to keep warm. Their needs are great, and so is their patience and humanity. I have so many stories to share, but for now I will share just 2 .⁽¹⁾.

Many have scabies (skin infestation of mites frequently becoming infected), so we have a makeshift area in the clinic where patients go to have medicated cream applied—males in one area and mothers and children in another. As you can imagine, towards the end of the day we are trying desperately to see and treat as many patients as possible, so the clinic gets very busy and full. There was a child, a man, and a woman waiting for scabies treatment. One of our team assumed that they were together, so she ushered them into an area and asked the adults to help put the cream on the child and then on each other in the "private and difficult to reach" spots. As it turned out, not only was the child not their child, but the man and the woman were not "together" either—they didn't even know each other! It was great comic relief to realize that we had asked perfect strangers to cover each other in lotion—especially after a very difficult, emotional day—and they all complied! I tell you this: I love Haitians and their ability to just roll with circumstances placed in front of them!

We saw many sick children, but early in the morning a mother with her infant was urgently brought into the clinic as soon as the linekeepers saw the child. The child's entire face, only sparing her eyelids, had been burned and was charred and crusted; her bed sheet had lit on fire from a fallen candle on the eve of the day we arrived. The small miracle lies in the fact that the rest of her body and her hair had not been burned and *that just a few minutes prior, we unintentionally found in the clinic the much-needed antibiotic burn cream in a very unlikely place. We were able to immediately care for this precious child, Melissa, with tenderness, compassion, tears in our eyes, and the right medications! We were also blessed with the wisdom and strength of both a social worker and psychotherapist on our team, who were ever so gentle with the raw feelings of this frightened young mother as they tended to her emotional needs. She revealed that she also had a newborn at home, and held the common Haitian belief that in order to save her young baby, she would need to give her burnt, injured child away. This small team of compassionate and empathetic professionals were able to guide this distraught mother's maternal bond back to her toddler daughter, Melissa, as we did burn care on her sweet daughter's face. The mom cradled her daughter affectionately as she walked home with Melissa clinging to her with both hands. The mom agreed to bring her back to the clinic tomorrow for more care.*

　　Please pray for those in need. We have many more days ahead of us.

Fondly,

Brian and Sue et al.

EMAIL: JANUARY 14, 2009

Hi again—

Tonight is our last night in Haiti for now. . . . We closed the week seeing almost 1,000 patients, and will provide de-worming medication for 600 more schoolchildren (and 20 team members!). We have seen many from the village, the surrounding villages, and villages several mountains over, who have carried their sick children for days back and forth to the clinic walking 5, 6, 7 hours or more each way. One family actually came from an 8-hour (one-way) trek back and forth twice in 2 days for a sick asthmatic child in order to receive nebulized albuterol and antibiotic injections!

　　Another family with a severely malnourished child returned several days later for us to see how much better the child was doing!!! This distance and their efforts are inconceivable to me and I truly cannot imagine the difficulty of this walk. I am grateful for our rudimentary but life-saving health care.

Conveying our emotions is very hard to do in such a short email . . . . We have so much to tell, many stories with so many special people behind those stories, and so many wonderful pictures. I think I'm going to set up a blog when I get home.

It seems like the level of sickness was higher this trip, but we had enough team members, medications, and a newly set-up lab to all work together for improved care for our Haitian friends.

We appreciate your participation in this mission through your gracious giving and helping, caring, and prayers. My hope is that you all somehow feel a part of our trip! We all have heavy hearts as we pack and prepare to come home—and it's not because of the snow and below-zero weather in Chicago waiting for us, but because there is so much more to do here!

God bless,
Sue and Brian and the rest
of the Little by Little team

7 | MAY–JUNE 2009: EDNAR

Si se Bondye ki voye. Li peya fre ou.
"If it is God who sends you, he'll pay your expenses."
—HAITIAN PROVERB

EMAIL: MAY 2009

Hi everyone—

Just a quick note to let you know that we arrived in Haiti safely with all our bags!!!

> *That's a first. Thanks for prayers—More tomorrow :)*
> *Brian and Sue*

EMAIL: MAY 26, 2009

Hey Mary—

We had a great day in clinic yesterday . . . .

> *Joanne and Jill are really working together nicely—the 2 of them are close to equaling one of YOU!!!!!! Brian and Jud are awesome up there too . . . so unpacking has gone well. Someone did a really nice job of organizing the storeroom, so Jill and Brian are REALLY happy campers! They say it's so great, they can find stuff and they can put stuff away. :) The waiting room is AMAZING!!!!!!! Everyone sits very orderly—and mesmerized by the TV—Willem LOVED the Veggie Tales and played it all day yesterday!!!!!! We started the day with a woman*

who collapsed outside clinic—it was pretty dramatic . . . and after a lot of chaos and upon further evaluation it is a consensus that she was faking . . . I'll tell you more later. :) It has been raining, and is raining, but we are all prepared. One of the little miracles that happened yesterday is that it wasn't raining on our way to clinic so we started the day dry. Then it stopped raining when it was time for lunch and we all got to the cafeteria dry; then it downpoured again literally as WE all got to the clinic and continued to downpour all afternoon, but then stopped at 4:00 as Willem was making us leave . . . . Anyway—more later—I have to get ready, we are doing PPD screening this A.M., and going to Pétionville school. :)

LOVE YOU!!!!!

Suz

EMAIL: MAY 27, 2009

Hi Marcia—

So just 2 unusual clinical stories so far . . . .

First thing in the morning, about 10 minutes after we walked into the clinic, a woman collapsed outside. After a big hubbub and a lot of drama, and a nice firm sternal rub, we decided that she was just trying to be first in line!

The clinical story is about Ednar, a man that is the caretaker for a house down the road here, who seems to be in congestive heart failure. Thready, pulse around 120, shortness of breath with mild grunting respirations with poor aeration and rales, low blood pressure barely 80/p, significant dependent pitting edema—in legs, penis, and scrotum, not able to lay down—he is sitting at the end of the bed with his scrotum hanging off the edge of the bed sweating like a cold glass of ice water—scanty urine output, decreased appetite. I gave him Lasix and some bananas. Came back at the end of the day and he had good urine output, his rales were almost gone, no more shortness of breath or grunting and ate a banana. He was still sitting on the end of the bed, despite my direction to sit back with legs up, so I moved him (with help from his wife). He was uncomfortable for about 5 minutes, then settled down and was back to being comfortable. So I left him like that last night; gave him more Lasix, applied support hose, and made a soft scrotal support from one of Brian's t-shirts. Will go back this A.M.

Wish you were here!

Sue

EMAIL: JUNE 2, 2009

It's the time of the morning when the crows are still active but the dogs have settled. I can hear the quiet sounds of the river, no longer angry with the rapid rush from the full and fast rains from the days prior. The sky has broken and I see the contrast of the beautiful Haitian blue peaking above the quilted green of the mountains. It's not yet bright—the sun has been very shy this trip, but the peace and calm of this moment remind me that this is God's way. We've experienced a week of high energy, resilience, and peace, with Haitian strength as our example. I am repeatedly amazed how a person suffering from anemia/malnutrition, along with an array of ailments, and a life of poverty and difficult weather can be so strong in body and heart. We will always have visions of parents and siblings carrying children over one or two mountains, through rocky, muddy, steep paths, waiting all day for medical care. We will remember the man with a year-old foot injury whose foot and ankle were swollen and his heel bone was exposed. He was wearing sandals that were pure trash. I remembered him from a year ago, when we saw and treated him with several antibiotics and antifungals, shaking our heads, thinking that he was surely going to lose his foot. We even had our doubts about him surviving this overwhelming infection, but yet here he was, a year later, telling us that he was better and thanking us for this care and a new pair of sandals. How did this man get to clinic? We can all barely handle walking up the mountainside with our healthy bodies and the best all-terrain shoes we can buy!

A few of us have been doing "home" visits twice a day to care for Ednar, an elderly man down the road from the guesthouse with congestive heart failure. He and his family live in a little square, concrete block room about 10 feet × 15 feet in size, with a concrete bed at one end of the room and a small table and crate chairs at the other, a dirt floor. This evening was my last visit with Ednar, and I was bringing him a present; my crank-wind flashlight that would never require batteries. He would always have light to see his medications and he would get exercise cranking the light up to work. As I approached Ednar's dwelling, I heard singing and moaning and there were at least 30 people crammed into his little house, all with eyes closed and hands swaying and reaching into the air. I tried to inch my way into the house to peek at Ednar. He was still in an upright position in his bed, head leaning against the wall, hands folded on his lap, in his white nightdress. Haitian prayer circles typically involve singing, a lead prayer, repetition of Bible verses, more singing, and then many people praying together over the person saying their own individualized prayer for that person. The leader then closes with another Bible verse or religious song. My heart sank and I felt totally distraught at the thought of Ednar dying during the day with everyone now singing him to heaven. Ednar's wife saw me with my sad expression, grabbed my hand, and pulled me close and yelled out, "Silence!" The chanting ceased. She brought me to Ednar and put my hand into Ednar's hand. He energetically opened his eyes, smiled at me with his toothless grin, relaxed his posture and started chatting in Creole about feeling better, thanking me, wanting me to see how he could walk as he got up from his bed to show me. I was literally dumbfounded. Of course I had thought he was dead, while they were all singing and praising that he was alive! Ednar and his wife were excited to complete our evening routine of taking his blood pressure, measuring his urine, receiving gifts of peanut butter and bananas with the extra gift of the flashlight. Ednar loved the "magic" flashlight! We exchanged our farewell hugs and then as quickly as he unfroze his position, he went back into his previous stiff posture, closed his eyes, and the chanting prayers resumed.

Your prayers and God's perfect timing have been evident throughout this trip, most specifically as our team pulled together yesterday. Our goal was to NOT leave the clinic with anyone not seen (every night we left with heavy hearts that 70–100 people would have to return the next day). We had a perfect plan—we became a well-oiled machine! We have seen many pregnant women, all doing amazingly well, so I was not surprised to see another sweet woman, looking about 7 months along, patiently waiting on the bench for her turn, her countenance calm. About a 1/2-hour later, I am told that her water bag very unexpectedly broke, and she was having contractions. We were not prepared to deliver a 26-week preemie . . . we cared for her as we waited for a truck to take her to the hospital. As a few of us traveled in the flatbed of the truck, over the wet, rough mountain roads, her contractions increased in frequency and intensity, passing the bloody mucus that indicates that delivery is imminent. But we made it, and she was quickly brought into the hospital. Through all of this, the rest of the team continued seeing patient after patient, and at the end of the day, each person waiting was seen. We never had a downpour, just some light rain that was actually refreshing after such a sweaty day.

Melissa, the 18-month-old who was so badly burned in January, was pure sunshine as her mother brought her back to see us. Miraculously the skin on her face was fully healed. She has scars, but not nearly to the extent we were anticipating. And most surprising is that the new skin is pigmented. She was toddling and smiling, well nourished, and her mom was absolutely beaming! The joy of these moments is really unexplainable.

We are packing up to leave for the airport, and with each wet, muddy piece of clothing we are putting into our suitcase, we are remembering each experience, each tear, each smile . . . if only we could pack up this Haitian strength, resilience, and peace!

Thank you all, over and over, for joining us on this journey. We have felt your interest, support, and prayers!

Brian and Sue and team

8 | JANUARY 2010: LITTLE THINGS

> *We ought not to be weary of doing little things for the love of God, who regards not the greatness of the work, but the love with which it is performed.*
> —BROTHER LAWRENCE

EMAIL: FRIDAY, JANUARY 8, 2010, 7:20 A.M.

Subject: Safe arrival

Hi from Haiti to snowy Chicago!!!

Thank you all for thinking of us and praying our safe way to Haiti. We (nurse practitioners: Dawn, Janice, Sharon, Sara, Therese, Tricia, Sue; nurse practitioner students: Anna, Amy, Heather, Sarah; team coordinator: Mary; Lab technician: Sandy; non-medical team assistants: Annette, Annie, Brian, David, James, Kristen, Patty, Stacey, Sparvim, Ray) have arrived WITHOUT a glitch . . . every person accounted for, EVERY bag miraculously weighed exactly 50 lbs (wink, wink) as we checked in at O'Hare, and each of those precious and peanut-butter-filled bags appeared on the PAP-side turnstile! We were out of the airport and up the mountain before dark—record time!

People were camped out waiting for our early morning arrival to the clinic. We had many preparatory meetings this year, so as we jumped off the trucks we were ready to go—well . . . a few walkers had to take a minute to wipe off their sweat (that is not a "no sweat" kind of climb).

We unloaded our nicely inventoried, numbered, and labeled suitcases (how impressive everyone was packing the Saturday before we left, finishing in less than 3 hours, BEFORE I even arrived!!!) and started seeing patients.

Our first patient was a tiny, elderly woman with the most radiant smile, calm disposition—wearing a stiff, old, thin, (gross) little blue dress. We learned from Willem that she had walked all day on Weds. and slept outside Weds. night. She was exuberant that she was our first patient! As her story unfolded to us and her clothes were removed, we saw an infection that was just absolutely raw and oozing, from her neck to her legs, truly the worst I have ever seen. We had no idea from her countenance the severity of her problem.

We tenderly bathed her, we gently applied medicated cream, we gave her a double shot of antibiotic in her thighs (the only place we could find that was without severe infection). We covered her in lovingly made soft blankets to keep her warm, we gave her peanut butter, Crocs, a health pack, vitamins, Brian's lunch, a soft T-shirt from a student's backpack . . . literally she was what every patient needed rolled into one. Throughout her painful treatment ordeal she kept smiling.

Many tears were shed with the large realization of the suffering—physical/emotional—that is "underneath," but with so many of us working together both here in Haiti and with all of you at home who have helped to send us here, we can relieve some of this suffering just a little bit at a time. She left with her husband by her side with a few tears gently gliding down her cheeks (the antibiotic shots hurting her legs? or the sweet tears of human connection?).

We were told by an interpreter that they would be walking for at least 12 hours and would be home by early morning. . . . It was cold and rainy here last night, but the clouds have cleared and the sun is peeking over the mountains. We are sure they are seeing the same sun on the other side of the mountain and that our little lady friend is feeling better today. :)

I hope you are seeing the sun sparkling in your yards and driveways this morning! We are thinking of all of you and are grateful for your prayers and support!

Brian and Sue

Email: Monday, January 11, 2010

Dear Friends—

As we get ready to pack to go home, we are looking at over 40 completely empty suitcases—and with each empty suitcase is a memory of an infant snuggled in a blanket and soft diaper; a child with colorful Crocs hugging his growing feet and a bar of soap to wash those feet; an adolescent with a toothbrush; a mother with a Band-Aid; so many infections and diseases treated with so many different medications; both the strong and weak slathered with creams to combat the intensity of an itsy-bitsy mite (scabies).

The amazement and pure joy in the return of a child who recovered from malnutrition through the determination of a father, eating a peanut butter porridge blend and many prayers. Severe burns and puncture wounds; sky-high blood pressure and beautiful mountains; pregnancy and death; teeth rotted to the root, smiles as wide as the river; healthy babies, people who don't know how old they are or their birthday; sharing sandwiches, shirts, and shoes, smiles and tears, human touch, humanity together in Haiti.

We are returning home after one more day in the clinic, with empty bags but full hearts! And as we will fill the bags again soon, our hearts will continue to overflow.

With gratitude and fondness,
Brian and Sue

> *Never part without loving words to think of during your absence. It may be that you will not meet again in this life.*
> —JEAN PAUL RICHTER

THE WEEK AT THE CLINIC WAS COMPLETE. OUR TEAM WAS FEELING VERY CONNECTED TO EACH OTHER, TO THE VILLAGERS, TO THE FAMILIES WHO WALKED SO FAR FOR SO LITTLE. WE ALL FELT AMAZINGLY SATISFIED. THE VILLAGERS HAD THEIR HEALTH PACKS, PAIN RELIEVERS, DE-WORMING MEDICATIONS, AND VITAMINS. IF THEY HAD AN INFECTION, THEY RECEIVED ANTIBIOTICS, WHETHER IN PILL FORM OR VIA AN INJECTION. IF THEY HAD HIGH BLOOD PRESSURE, THEY GOT MEDICATION TO SAFELY KEEP THE HYPERTENSION IN CHECK. IF THEY HAD *"l'acide,"* THEN TUMS OR A STRONGER ANTACID WAS PRESCRIBED. ALL THE PREGNANT MOMS HEARD THE MIRACLE SOUND OF THEIR BABY'S HEARTBEAT, ALL THE *mamba* (PEANUT BUTTER) WE HAD LEFT WAS DISTRIBUTED, EVERY last lovingly hand-sewn blanket found a baby to cuddle, and each pair of Crocs left the clinic on happy feet.

There was no salt left to pass out; that is, the fortified salt that we had just started to distribute to all families who come to the clinic to help eradicate a condition called lymphatic filariasis, which is more commonly known as *elephantitis*. The symptoms of swollen extremities and very engorged scrotum occur when the filarial worm settles and becomes lodged in the lymphatic system, clogging the lymphatic drainage system, leading to the affected legs having an elephant-like appearance, along with significant discomfort. I have seen legs so swollen there is no ankle definition and scrotums so swollen they are the size of melons, heavy and very difficult to support. I can't imagine having this condition on top of all the other discomforts of the Haitian lifestyle. We hope that the combination of a medication called albendazole and this new fortified salt will not only eradicate this disease, but also introduce essential iodine into the Haitians' diet to help prevent thyroid goiters. We have to teach the Haitian salt users not to wash the salt. *"No lave!"* we warn, so they don't inadvertently wash away all the essential additives to the salt. It had to be explained to me that the Haitians are used to cooking with rock salt, which is dirty and has to be cleaned before it can be added to food. There are so many simplicities we take for granted in the United States, a country of clean, fortified salt and no filarial worms.

The microscope in the lab that guided our treatment for multiple sexually transmitted infections (STIs) throughout the week was carefully packed up. The other lab reagents, which accurately diagnosed urinary tract infections, anemia, malaria, tuberculosis, and HIV, were also packed, to be stored in the guesthouse refrigerator with the tetanus vaccines and other biologicals that must be kept cool. We brought these reagents back and forth to the clinic every day in coolers with ice packs to maintain their efficacy, as there is no electricity in the clinic. We were all in such a happy yet uncertain state of mind as we continued to pack up and clean up our patient examination stations, visualizing and remembering the patients we had each seen and treated throughout the week, imprinting them in our memory banks, to learn more and seek out advice from colleagues at home to bring back further treatment plans. But even more importantly, we wanted to purposefully remember each patient as an individual, as an equal human being, to try to come to grips with why they were born into such physical discomforts of extreme poverty, and we were born into such lavish, everyday extravagances of food, water, shelter, and safety.

We gathered our end-of-day reports, which will be tallied to give us a total of all the patients seen throughout the week, along with their ages, gender, and diagnosis/problems and prescriptions dispensed. This helps us plan for future teams, for the needed supplies and medications, and to see the trends of maladies and diseases we are seeing over the years. We also keep track of the villages where the patients come from, many being from villages where distance is measured by how many mountains are crossed and/or whether part of the walk is by moonlight. I always feel unsettled when I find out at the end of a clinic day that time ran out before we had a chance to see everyone who had been waiting. Frequently, more than 100 people are given little pieces of paper with numbers for the following day to be "first" in line. They will sleep outside, somewhere around the clinic, under the brush, the moon and stars, amidst mosquitoes and frequently wind and rain. Sometimes they have already slept outside the night before, as they were traveling overnight to the clinic, and will have to do the same going home. Often not feeling well themselves, they carry sick and hungry children, enduring the hardships of the elements with no bathrooms and no showers.

Uncomfortable thoughts like these burden me and sometimes drain my strength at the end of the day. Photographs are not necessary. My brain has permanent imprints of each patient and malady I've seen or heard about. I've tried to leave heavy baggage like this behind in the clinic. It doesn't work. I've found, however, that the mind and heart pain that comes with dragging each heavy load along with me from home, clinic, and in life actually gives me energy, desire, memory, and ideas with an intensity I'm certain could not be duplicated had I not endured and gained strength from carrying all that baggage.

My spiritual growth also abounds.

As I'm reviewing my end-of-week log sheet, I flash back to the first days of clinic and remember a young girl from the village school who was five years old. She had her shabby but clean yellow pinafore uniform dress on, with her hair in the classic ponytails with two big yellow ribbons, beautiful shy brown eyes, and a warm, timid smile. She was hanging around the clinic after school, as so many of the school children do. They love to just watch, catching glimpses of our busy, almost frenetic work. They stand or sit and look and smile. Sometimes they kick around an empty pill bottle or some other makeshift soccer ball. I wonder what they are thinking about while watching us *"blancs"* (whites) as we scurry around like drones in a hive, all of us trying desperately to make the bitterness we taste as we see their lean lives seem to sweeten up just a bit from our small efforts.

Gerda was hanging with the rest as I came out with some old plastic grocery bags. I was planning on gathering the kids together to pick up the garbage left on the ground from so many people milling around all week. I was prepared to trade garbage for peanut butter, and despite my broken Creole, they understood me perfectly well, and now were moving with a purpose. Even Gerda came to me for a bag, but as she walked toward me, I noticed her right arm dangling as she reached for the garbage bag with her left. She cautiously and tenderly looped the bag over this limp hand, so she could use her functioning hand to pick up the garbage. This certainly caught my attention, and as I looked more closely, I noticed that her left hand was red and swollen. I guided her into the clinic, again speaking short Creole phrases which she understood. I asked her if her hand and arm hurt; she just smiled. I asked her how long her arm has been looking like this, how this happened; and again, she just smiled. She had a high fever, but she didn't seem to be aware, and didn't answer me when I asked her how long she had been hot. I could not find a break or sign of injury in her skin, and I was afraid she had a bone infection. I told her I was going to give her medicine to get rid of the infection, that it would only work if I gave it to her as an injection. She again seemed to understand, but just smiled, petting my arm like a sweet old lady would pet her lap dog.

I didn't want to leave her alone, so one of the nurses prepared the injection for me, mixing the antibiotic with an injectable numbing medicine so that as the stinging antibiotic penetrated the muscle it wouldn't hurt quite so much. There was too much medicine to give in one shot, so rather than giving one injection and then another, we tag-teamed and gave her two pokes simultaneously on the count of three. She barely flinched. As soon as we finished, gave her hugs and a Tootsie Pop, she asked if she could go now to collect garbage because she really wanted some peanut butter. I explained that I wanted her to rest her arm for the rest of the day, and that I really needed and wanted her to come back tomorrow for me to check on her, and to bring one of her parents. It was Friday and there would be no school on Saturday, so I was not certain if this important follow-up would actually happen.

I gave her peanut butter as I made the "shush" sign with my finger across my lips, and asked her if she understood. I didn't want the other children who were collecting the garbage in exchange for peanut butter to see that she had received her peanut butter "for free." Again the adorable smile persisted, her eyes sparkling with comprehension. She put her peanut butter and lollipop in her garbage bag, and ran right past the other children—to where, I wasn't sure. My guess would be somewhere secluded to enjoy her Tootsie Pop, and then home to share her peanut butter with her family. The intake nurses and my husband got a good look at Gerda, so if they noticed her on Saturday, they would bring her in to clinic for her second round of injections. I wasn't surprised when she showed up on Saturday outside the clinic with her garbage bag. I was sad that she was alone. However, to my delight, her hand was less swollen and less red; her fever was low grade and she was ready for another couple of injections, another Tootsie Pop, and more peanut butter. She came again on Sunday with her bag in tow for the same. She no longer had a fever, and her hand was looking excellent. Her smile was contagious. She was still asking to collect garbage for peanut butter. By Monday I was able to speak with her teacher, instructing the teacher to give her an oral antibiotic daily for the following week. Her infection was going to resolve. Oh, Gerda, how precious you are!

10 | Double Flashback: Richard

> *You must look into other people*
> *as well as at them.*
> —Lord Chesterfield

It's Tuesday, January 12, 2010, just after 4:00 p.m.; I am starting to see the end-of-the-week "flashbacks" as I move through the clinic. I'm taking my inventory tour. Supply check, missioner check (to see if anyone has depleted a supply that will be essential for the next team), taking pencil-and-paper notes along with my perpetual mental notepad. As I'm making my rounds, I can't help but recall Richard, a 13-year-old boy who found his way to the clinic on the first day of our arrival. Three days prior, a kerosene lamp had exploded in his face.

There he was, hovering by the clinic wall, face turned downward, shoulders rounded and stooped in a position to shadow his face from the baking sun, with his shirt pulled up over his neck and ears. He was apparently alone, and he had no dossier number to be in line. Because his posture was so unusual, he was noticed fairly quickly by our intake team and was brought to my attention. When I caught a glimpse of his face, I realized that it was really black. Not the beautiful, shiny, smooth black of the typical Haitian skin, but a charcoal-charred black, like that of a log rescued from a bonfire. His eyelids were so very swollen, I don't think he could blink, and I imagined he could barely see. There were shiny wet spots near the corners of his eyes. His lips were also swollen, and were taut, cracked, and bleeding. His entire face was burned. I thought to myself, "Oh, what agony he must be in. How do I keep myself from crying?" I didn't. I had the same wet spots in the corners of my eyes, which blurred my vision. It was OK. I knew my way around the clinic—I also knew my way around the pain of a severely burned face. I suddenly experienced the double flashback phenomenon, picturing the miracle of Melissa's face while cradling Richard. Richard's and Melissa's countenances morphed together and became one in my mind. I saw hope, I saw repair. I saw renewal instead of pain, despair, and dead ash.

I told Richard in Creole that I would take care of him, and I led him back to my little spot in the corner of the clinic near a large window, which provides me excellent light. While still talking in my limited vocabulary of Creole, my first question to Richard was, "Have you had anything to eat today?" Not surprisingly, his answer was a quiet "No." I asked him to please take a few bites of my peanut butter sandwich, explaining that I wanted to give him a strong pain medication, but that it shouldn't be taken on an empty stomach. He did as I requested, as I picked a small bite off the sandwich with my fingers and placed it very slowly past his burnt lips and into his mouth. He chewed gingerly and was quite eager to drink the water given to him to wash down the medication. He drank as carefully and slowly as he chewed. He drooled the water out of his mouth and had trouble getting down the pain medication, but he eventually successfully swallowed. When I asked him to lie down, he did so, but hesitantly. I then noticed that he also had burns on the palms and dorsa of his hands, and it likely hurt to support the weight of his trunk on his hands as he reclined. I commanded, but in a soft soothing voice, "*Lashe, lashe. Dacore, dacore.*" [Relax, relax. It will be OK.] I cooed these two words over and over as I petted his shoulder. I thought hearing my voice saying Creole words would help him to trust. His tense muscles gave way as I gave him a light massage. Next, I had to explain to him that I would make him feel better, but that the process would hurt. I needed to tell him that I would be gentle, I would be loving, I would give him more medicine to help him through the pain if he needed it. I also wanted to reassure him that he should tell me if he was frightened, or if the pain was intolerable. I really needed a translator!

It was our first day of clinic, and our translators were establishing themselves. I asked for assistance because my Creole is so limited and, via the busy translator, I explained to Richard the burn debridement process. The translator left to help another provider. I could tell that Richard was frightened. He was still and stoic, very cooperative, but his body language was tensed up again. One of our team members, Mary, gathered the needed supplies. I started by soaking paper towels in a sterile saline solution. I carefully and slowly placed each wet towel gently onto the thick burnt skin of his face, eyelids, ears, lips, and tip of his nose. He was relaxing and doing well until I put a wet towel onto a large crusty scab on the tip of his nose. He immediately became agitated and sat upright, causing all of the carefully placed, clean, wet towels to fall onto the filthy floor. I didn't realize at the time that he must have experienced a sense of claustrophobia, a mini-water-boarding experience, that truly had to be torture for him. I felt really bad. I got the interpreter again, and had him ask how Richard was doing. Richard couldn't speak well: his lips were too injured, too tight to move enough to form words. The interpreter and I explained the whole process again, but this time I was more careful to be sure that I did not cover any part of his nostrils with the soaked towels. He continued to lie there still as a mummy, just shaking his head either slightly up and down or back and forth to answer my questions. "Can you breathe OK? Are you in pain? Are you scared? Do you want another bite of peanut butter sandwich?" Mary was holding his hand, stroking his arm, using her mother-love voice, chirping beautiful things, imagining her own son lying there . . . the wet spots are falling all around her eyes now too. We couldn't look at each other, or we would both have lost it.

I worked on removing as much dead skin as I could, my saline water smoky black, with bits of charcoal skin both floating and sinking in the basin. His facial skin had a little bleeding, which was a sign of viability, a sense of crimson hope. I applied a white antibiotic cream to every area of the burn, producing a ghastly, ghostly appearance of his face and hands, made worse with an application of gauze in mummy fashion, made even more disturbing by adding a hat, sunglasses, and a new backpack filled with supplies. Now Richard reminded me of the old black-and-white movie version of *The Invisible Man*—which was a much better visual than the initial startle of mummies and ghosts, especially in Haiti, the land of voodoo. At this point, Stephan, the missionary's 13-year-old son, found Richard and me, curious as to what was going on. I told him the story, and it turned out that the two teens knew each other. Richard used to attend the missionary's school in the past. Stephan thought Richard was once expelled from school for fighting. Stephan was cheerful and thoughtful, and immediately connected with Richard, speaking jovially to him. I actually saw, under the gauze wrap, the corners of Richard's lips lift slightly into what could be construed as a smile in response to Stephan. I asked Stephan to continue to chat with Richard while I went to get his antibiotic injections.

Stephan was now my perfect translator. He was kind and empathetic and saying all the right things, without my prompting. He explained the antibiotic shots and the Tootsie Pop. Richard lay prone on the table, exposing his buttocks, readying himself for our double needles. We gave Richard his injections in our well-practiced "1, 2, 3, go" tag-team technique, and he didn't flinch. Stephan reiterated to him how amazingly brave he was, and how he was very much admired for being so strong. Then Stephan started to tell him Melissa's story: How one year ago, a little girl in the village who was only 1½ years old got the same bad burns on her face. She was sleeping on a blanket on the floor and a candle got knocked over; it fell on the blanket, the blanket lit up with fire, and burned her face as well. Stephan told Richard that I had taken care of Melissa and that she had done really well, that all of her skin grew back and that she "looked real good and was feeling real fine." Richard responded with an empty nod.

With Stephan's help, I implored Richard to return the next day for his much-needed second treatment. I promised him another peanut butter sandwich and Tootsie Pop. Then a miracle happened. As we were escorting Richard out of the clinic, Melissa and her mom were walking into the clinic. Stephan noticed Melissa first and called out to Richard, *"Garde! Garde!* [Look! Look!] This is the little girl I was telling you about with the burned face. Look how healthy and wonderful she is!! That will be you, too!" God's timing for the two to meet in person at that exact moment was perfect. They had already met in my mind hours before. Richard quietly told Stephan he would be waiting for me at the clinic wall first thing the next morning, and that God gave him hope.

By this time, with all of our exuberance spilling into the clinic over the meeting of Richard and Melissa, my husband, Brian, came to see what was happening. He asked Stephan if he knew where Richard lived. Stephan thought he lived all the way up and over the mountain to the north, and explained that it would be a couple hours' walk. Brian and Stephan quickly decided to take Richard up the north mountain, the three of them on the four-wheeler. They reached Richard's house after an hour of baking in the hot, dry, parching sun. The two then returned tired and drenched with sweat, wondering how Richard would do this trek back and forth, on foot, by himself for the next five days.

11 | ROCKS

BEYOND THAT FIRST MOUNTAIN, THERE ARE OTHER MOUNTAINS: STEEP MOUNTAINS, WITH MORE ROCKS, NO EASY SOURCE OF WATER, MORE CHILDREN, MORE NEEDS, AND MORE KINDS OF INFECTIONS—ESPECIALLY INTESTINAL WORMS, WHICH ALSO REQUIRE EXPENSIVE MEDICATION TO PROVIDE AN EFFECTIVE TREATMENT. I'VE FELT MISERABLE, TO THE POINT OF TEARS, WHEN I'VE HAD THE STOMACH FLU IN THE PAST. WHEN I'M SICK, ALL I WANT IS THE COMFORT OF MY BATHROOM WITH ALL ITS AMENITIES: A CLEAN PORCELAIN TOILET, CUSHY TOILET PAPER, FLUFFY FACIAL TISSUE, A FRESH SOFT WASHCLOTH, MOUTH-WASH—YET I STILL FEEL SORRY FOR MYSELF IF I VOMIT OR HAVE REPEATED BOUTS OF DIARRHEA. I CAN'T EVEN IMAGINE WHAT IT WOULD FEEL LIKE TO BE BLOATED, NAUSEATED, AND WEAK DAY AFTER LONG day filled with the effects of intestinal parasites or gastroenteritis on top of worms. These impoverished Haitians have no running water, no plumbing, no crackers or bubbly lemon-lime soda pop, no clean washcloth, no day off from work. Instead, they have to continue working in the heat on the mountainside for survival, caring for children who are healthy or sick, going outside for the "toilet" in the brush, vomiting and passing sickening worms into a bucket and discarding the smelly grossness of it—who knows where.

Everyone continued packing and organizing the clinic supplies; packing their own personal supplies, cameras, otoscopes, stethoscopes; packing up all of their memories and the emotions they had experienced on this miraculous mountaintop. After our inventory and packing were completed and our garbage had been collected, and after we had made sure that all waiting patients had been seen, we were ready to leave the clinic. Almost everyone, sparing just a few, decided to take a slow walk back to the guesthouse, soaking up the green of the terraced farms growing vegetables such as leeks and cabbages, holding hands with some friendly, outgoing village children who were excited to guide them down the rocky, curvy mountain paths. The echoing *"Bonsoir, bonsoir! A biento!!"* [Good evening, good evening! Next time!!] cascaded down the mountain as traveler and villager enthusiastically greeted each other, as their paths crossed for a brief moment. As the walkers came to the dry riverbed, many searched for a heart-shaped white river rock—surprisingly, not that difficult to find—as a tangible, hold-in-your-hand remembrance of this special mountain jewel in Haiti, where each missioner met so many amazingly special people. God has been good to all.

Rocks have always been an apropos symbol of Haiti to me. The Haitian side of the island of Hispaniola is almost all rocky, mountainous terrain. There are rocks everywhere. They twist ankles when stepped on, they scrape elbows when fallen on, and can become weapons when thrown. In the villages, people work the ground, harvesting rocks from the soil, then tilling the bits of soil by hand in preparation for their vegetables. Rocks and more rocks seem to re-grow in the fields, displacing the hunger-dispelling, life-saving crops, mauling the carefully planted and tended gardens. Farmers, male and female, young and old, seem to dig up more rocks than potatoes, carrots, beets, or onions.

Rocks are a mixed blessing. They can be hand-pounded to create a crumble small enough to mix with sand and a concrete fixative, to be poured into handmade molds that are then set out in the baking sun to make brick blocks. The worker can also pummel the rock crumble to an even finer texture, again to be mixed with a fixative to produce mortar to hold the bricks together, then stacked and cemented into small square huts or even a substantially large building; these make strong shelters against sun and rain. Most village settlements are constructed with these handmade bricks. The abodes have dirt floors and concrete beds and are only one story. Rooms are separated by brick blocks. Blue tarps or corrugated plastic are used for roofing. To construct a concrete or brick roof, or a larger dwelling, one needs connecting support, which requires the use of scarce rebar or expensive and elusive steel. Thus, roofs are simply and cheaply made of tarps and corrugated plastic, or there just are no roofs. Torn bed sheets, ragged blankets, or the occasional prized bit of cardboard are draped over or secured to the brick to provide spotty cover from the sun or rain. Clotheslines sag from brick side to brick side, adding flashing color to the house like dispirited strings of advertising flags on a no-longer-new storefront.

Very little wood or lumber is available for building material or furniture. Wood is not a natural resource. Haiti has been severely deforested—so much so that I have seen an aerial picture of the island of Hispaniola with an obvious demarcating line between the Dominican Republic and Haiti, created by the stark contrast between green and barren, trees and no trees. When charcoal can't be found for cooking or for a heat fire, the only alternatives are to cut down a tree, whether it's old or yearling; or to burn furniture, whether it's junk or fine. There are no gas stoves, there are no appliances, and there is no electricity. Open fires are a way of life and survival. They are also the portal for eye irritation, nasal congestion, asthma, burns that cause severe injury, and the reason for the ravaged environment.

Each mountain has many burdens, but also many joys. A mountain sunrise and a mountain sunset are not only spectacularly gorgeous, but also can signify another day of life with a loved one. Rocks and mountains are the foundations for village after village. When a mountain waterfall or stream is discovered, it can be very clean, renewing, and reviving. A petite pink flower will subtly pop out of a dry rock; a large trumpet vine will blast out that life is beautiful and that both life and health are not elusive or impossible.

All of this and more can be symbolized by one little rock. The heart-shaped rock a homeward-bound visitor finds resonates to a depth deeper than bone, down to the visitor's viscera; especially if that visitor was in Haiti during the earthquake.

PART TWO

THE EARTHQUAKE

EMAIL: TUESDAY,
JANUARY 12, 2010, 5:12 P.M.

From: Sue Walsh

Subject: Hello Everyone!

We want to get the word out to as many people as possible that we are all OK after experiencing a very large earthquake here in Haiti.

There is much damage here, but again, we are OK and so is the house we are staying in. We will contact you as soon as we can. We are due to leave tomorrow, but we will have to see how the roads are and if the airport is open. Not sure of communication abilities. Please pray for our Haitian friends and keep them close to your hearts.

Sue

12 | FIRST HOUR

*Find rest, oh my soul, in God alone; my hope comes
from Him. He alone is my rock and my salvation.*
—PSALM 62: 5–6

BRIAN AND I AND A FEW OTHERS STAYED BACK IN
THE CLINIC AS EVERYONE ELSE MEANDERED DOWN
THE MOUNTAIN. WE WERE TICKING OFF OUR CHECK-
LIST, MAKING SURE OF THIS AND THAT. IT WAS OUR
USUAL PLAN TO TAKE THE FOUR-WHEELERS BACK TO
THE GUESTHOUSE, WHICH WAS A SPEEDY JOURNEY
BACK AND FORTH, ALLOWING US ALWAYS TO BE THE
LAST TO LEAVE AND THE FIRST TO ARRIVE. THIS WAS
WHAT I VIEWED AS ESSENTIAL FOR OUR LEADER-
SHIP, GIVING US THE ABILITY TO ALWAYS KNOW THE
LOCATION OF EACH TEAM MEMBER AND TO PERSON-
ALLY FEEL THE PULSE OF THE SITUATION FIRST AND
LAST. IT WAS A SPECTACULAR DAY WITH SUNSHINE,
BLUE SKY, AND A LOVELY CARIBBEAN BREEZE. AS WE
BUMPED AND JOGGED DOWN THE HILL ON THE FOUR-
WHEELED ATV, WE CROSSED THE DRY RIVER AND

sped up the road to the guesthouse. We greeted and waved to our team members, who were mingling with the now very familiar villagers. Of course we were sad that our week of service had ended, but we were also excited to be heading back to Chicago, to our families and friends, our jobs and computers, our lingering showers, regular clothes, familiar favorite foods, and our own beds.

By the time we reached the guesthouse, two women from our team had already gotten there and occupied both bathrooms; they were purposely first in the line of 21 others to take their farewell "Haitian bath," consisting of water in a plastic bin, a pitcher to direct the water to the spot needing to become wet or rinsed, and a musty towel. Primitive and inadequate as it may sound, all of this was a great source of refreshment after working and sweating in the dusty heat of Haiti all day. It was around 4:45 P.M. and Brian and I were starting to organize our 46 suitcases to be readied for our return flight home. We were chatting while walking in and out of the house. We were carrying the beat-up, broken suitcases, which were not worth the hassle of bringing home, outside to the patio; inside we were lining up the suitcases that were in good enough condition to accompany us back to Chicago. At that moment, exactly 4:53 P.M. Haitian time, there was a huge, huge, huge sound which had the magnified quality of multiple fast, rumbling trains overhead (a familiar sound in Chicago from the infamous "El" traveling quickly on the elevated tracks that run over the city). That sound developed from nowhere, while simultaneously all of the floors and walls of the house severely shook and shifted, giving me the impression in my split-second assessment that everything around me was going to explode.

I shouted with the full strength of my voice while running up the stairs, pounding on the doors to the girls in the bathrooms to "Get out, get out!! The house is exploding!" I ran downstairs and out to the front yard, thinking that I was just in time to watch the whole dwelling collapse, frantic that my friends were not yet out of the bathrooms. The trees in the yard were rhythmically swaying back and forth, branches touching ground with each shift, as if 150-mile-an-hour winds in a hurricane or tornado were causing the bend of the branches. There was no wind. The sky could not have been bluer. There was no rain. The deafening noise was persisting, the house was moving back and forth, the girls were not coming out! I ran back in, screaming, screaming again for them to "GET OOOUUUT!! PLEEEASE! The house is EXPLOOOOOODING!!" Brian also ran around the house trying to figure out what was exploding. Was it the cisterns on the roof, or the propane tanks? Had a truck or airplane exploded or crashed? What could he find to prevent the roof from collapsing? But the excruciatingly loud noise and confusingly persistent rumbling, shaking, and shifting persisted for almost a minute—much, much longer than any explosion or crash would have continued.

Finally, the slow-motion-like minute came to a sudden halt. There were no sounds. The guesthouse was no longer moving. The trees stopped bending. Everything was still standing upright. There had been no explosion. No one was hurt. The walkers who had been on the last leg of their walk home bounded past the front gate of the guesthouse, short of breath and panicked. They had been running and falling uphill, on the shaking and shifting road, away from an avalanche that was propelling rocks down the mountainside and completely pummeling the riverbed. They darted past the shifting, shaking, tumbling walls and houses on the road. "It's an earthquake, there's been an earthquake!" everyone was yelling. We were all talking at once, but coming to the same conclusion. There *had* been an earthquake, one of gigantic proportions! I immediately went into the familiar "find your buddy now" mode, while each person, equally concerned about the well-being of the assigned counterpart for the trip, sought out his or her buddy. Our entire team was located and accounted for. Our host family was also located and accounted for. We were literally counting our blessings.

Brian and Willem immediately decided that a few of us should go back up to the village to see if anyone was hurt. Before I grabbed my backpack and my willing friends Dawn and David, I went to the computer and saw, in baffled disbelief, that the Internet connection was functioning, I typed out a short message to my kids and immediate family that there had been an earthquake in Haiti, but reassured them that we were all safe and fine. The six of us then ran outside to the four-wheelers and hightailed it back up the mountain, following the path set by Willem and Johanne, his amazing assistant. The avalanche came into view on the far side of the mountain, looking as if that side of the mountain had indeed exploded. Giant white boulders were strewn amongst tons of less sizeable rocks, exposing the inside of the mountain like the bone in a deep laceration. The walkers told us that during the earthquake, they first surmised that the loud noise and the ground shifts and shakes were caused from several large trucks driving down the mountain behind them. As the ground continued to rumble and the freight-train-like noise accelerated, they scrambled over unstable ground, twisting around, to get out of the way of the trucks they imagined were right behind them. As they looked backward, the familiar green mountain became a backdrop for the surreal: a visual and audio overload as they witnessed the typically lush mountainside crumble apart and tumble hard and fast into the riverbed. A fluffy, white, mushroom-like plume rose from the riverbed midway up the mountain, creating an illusion like Niagara Falls—only the falls were rock and the mist cloud was chalky dust. They saw no trucks, which of course changed their explanation for what they had just experienced. Initially, their mistaken conclusion was that the avalanche had caused the ground instability, until Mary, a native Californian, yelled out, "It's an earthquake! A BIG earthquake!"

We continued up the road to the village, people running out to greet us, talking rapidly in frightened Creole, taking us to several crumbled concrete dwellings, to a few villagers with cuts and bruises. No one had a severe injury. Only a dozen or so houses were completely ruined, and all dwellers had gotten out before their houses collapsed. We went through most of the village, making certain of everyone's status, again recognizing God's blessings over and over in the safety of each family. We decided that we needed to head down the mountain to check the riverbed before it got too dark. It was January, and it was already dusk by that time. As we came to the riverside, we saw a man walking toward us. Willem asked him if he knew of anyone who had been hurt by the avalanche. The man told us that he knew of no one who was hurt. What a miracle! This appeared to us to be a very big earthquake of high seismic proportions, in addition to being the first earthquake in the past 200 years of Haitian history. It also seemed that there was only minimal damage to property and no severe injuries to persons. We were so relieved.

We crossed the riverbed, and had just perched ourselves on a small plateau to view the entirety of the avalanche when we saw a man running toward us over the white rocks of the dry river. He was carrying a small person, whose limbs flopped like a tousled rag doll with each hurried step he took. He had no shirt on and as he came closer to us we could see that his shirt was turbaned around this young girl's head— and the shirt was a soaked red. Rapid Creole words were exchanged between Willem and this distressed man. Willem then asked me to examine the young girl, Katia, the man's daughter. She was five years old and was a student at the village school. She had gotten caught in the falling rocks of the avalanche. Dawn and I walked over to the man and his daughter, almost tripping over our own feet in our haste, and immediately assessed Katia to be unconscious. We could tell she had a severe head injury even before we removed the makeshift turban. She was lifelessly limp, but I could hear the coarseness of her breathing; obviously mucus or vomit was accumulating in her throat. The father's shirt on Katia's head was drenched with his daughter's blood, mingling with the sweat of his daily toil. I looked at Willem with an empathetic demeanor and told him that her condition was grave, and there was an urgent need for emergency care. Our team was scheduled to leave early the following morning, so there would be no possibility for care beyond tonight. We thought it best to take Katia to the nearest hospital, a short mountain-road distance away. I realized that this emergency transport would not be on a nice paved urban street, in an ambulance, with a priority pathway made by all who heard the siren and saw the flashing lights.

As I sat behind David on the four-wheeler, facing up the mountain with our backs to the river, Katia was placed carefully in my lap. Her dad eased onto the seat behind me, grabbing my waist tightly as Willem tried to give driving directions to David. The exchange of directions was taking too long. Willem was suddenly distracted by a faint sound, as he simultaneously noticed, out of the corner of his eye, dozens of people in the distance. They were advancing up the dry river. He could sense there was another significant need heading toward him. He finally and curtly directed us to just head up the mountain and motioned that Katia's dad would tell us where to turn, "*a doit ou a gouch*," meaning right or left. David started the all-terrain vehicle, as I turned backward to look at Brian. The vehicle jolted forward at that moment, and we sped away, up the now-darkening mountain. Katia lay still and heavy across my legs, her neck cradled in my left arm, her knees bent and secure over my right arm. I was wedged between David, who was holding tightly to the handlebars of the ATV, steering us madly toward the hospital, and Katia's dad, who was snugly hugging my middle, murmuring softly into the cool night air. With each bump and turn, I was acutely aware that my hands were full. I had nothing and no one to hold onto to stabilize my position on the fast-moving four-wheeler except Katia, with my quivering knees grasping the saddle of the ATV. I knew at that point I had to have full faith that God had purposefully put David into the driver's seat. He was a well-seasoned police officer, with a calm demeanor and lots of driving experience.

We left Brian, Willem, Dawn, and Johanne behind by the riverbed, as David, Katia, Katia's dad, and I sped away. The group we left behind planned to head back to the guesthouse to see if there was any other news about the earthquake and await a call from us once we got to the hospital. Coming from the recesses of the rocks, they heard a faint chanting, which became progressively louder and clearer and nearer. The singing was becoming distinct enough to grab their attention and slow their remounting of the ATVs. They eventually saw a procession of about 50 villagers heading toward them. The villagers were walking and swaying, reaching their arms into the darkening sky while a few strong men carried an older woman on a wooden chair with armrests above their heads, like a queen on a throne in a parade. As this vision came closer, they were able to see that the woman on the chair was injured. When the processional was upon them, they could also see that the woman looked like she had no face. The skin on her face was peeled back sideways and down, from her cheek, down the side of her nose, through her upper and lower lips and her chin. The flapping and bleeding skin exposed her facial bones and her teeth like a skeleton. Her moans floated upward with the villagers' chants as she was carried across the river and up the mountain to the lookout plateau where Brian, Willem, Dawn, and Johanne were still standing. The processional moved as one up the mountain, passing right by the four standing in awe. It appeared that the people's intent was to walk this revered village elder all the way to the hospital, in the dark. Brian, Dawn, Willem, and Johanne, as they headed back to the guesthouse, respectfully slowed and quieted their ATVs and ducked their heads as they carefully passed by the group. Willem was clearly unnerved, and was already forming a plan to help the elder woman to the hospital. Leaving Brian to settle and relax everyone at the guesthouse, Willem sought out the entourage in his pickup truck, eventually convincing a few villagers to put the injured woman in her chair in the back of the truck. He wanted to get to the hospital not only to help this poor woman, but also to see how we were doing with Katia.

13 | SECOND HOUR

> *I expect to pass through life but once. If, therefore,*
> *there be any kindness I can show, or any good thing*
> *I can do to any fellow being, let me do it now, for*
> *I shall not pass this way again.*
> —WILLIAM PENN (1644)

DAVID SKILLFULLY AND SPEEDILY WEAVED AROUND ROCKS, SLOW-MOVING TRUCKS, AND ONCOMING VEHICLES UP THE DARK MOUNTAIN TOWARD THE HOSPITAL. KATIA WAS UNRESPONSIVE AND LIMP, AND HER BREATHING WAS NOISY, RAPID, AND SHALLOW. IT WAS EVIDENT THAT SHE WAS DROWNING IN HER OWN SECRETIONS. I REALIZED THAT I HAD TO CLEAR KATIA'S AIRWAY OF THE PHLEGM AND FLUIDS WHICH WERE ACCUMULATING IN HER UPPER AIRWAY. IF I DIDN'T DO THIS SOON, THERE WOULD BE NO NEED TO RACE TO THE HOSPITAL. I COCKED HER HEAD SLIGHTLY BACK, TOOK A DEEP, DEEP BREATH, AND BLEW A HARD, FAST BREATH INTO HER OPENED MOUTH. THE SALTY MUCUS CAME BLASTING OUT OF HER NOSE, ONTO MY FACE AND INTO MY MOUTH, STARTLING ME INTO REALIZING THAT MY HANDS were fully occupied, and that I could not wipe my face or my mouth. I leaned forward and spit out the mucus and wiped my face as best I could on the back of David's shirt. He just kept driving. I did this several more times, recalling my snorkeling days, trying to muster the strength for the short, fast mouth-to-snorkel blow, clearing Katia's airway with the same intensity that I would clear my own airway when diving into the beauty and calm of a coral reef. Katia's airway cleared after four or five successive "blows," and she started to take deeper, better breaths. I was grateful that the secretions were only mucus; they could have been mixed with vomit.

We continued our fast trek to the hospital, dodging all kinds of unexpected obstacles on the dark road. Every minute or two, I administered another clearing air blast into Katia's mouth, successfully easing her breathing with more skill each time. I've done CPR before, but never on a moving vehicle with no hands, no equipment, and no help. My arm, leg, and back muscles were amazingly strong. I suppose, in retrospect, that strength came from the effects of an adrenaline rush. I was ironically glad that I had not eaten since breakfast and that I had had very little to drink all day. Otherwise, I surely would have vomited on myself and peed in my pants.

We arrived at the hospital after . . . I don't know how long. David sprang off the four-wheeler and offered his arms for Katia so that I could dismount also. I was being protective now, showing David exactly how to hold the t-shirt turban with compression on Katia's head, while at the same time balancing the exact angle to position her neck so she could breathe—and barking all of this at David as we ran in tandem into the hospital. Katia's dad slid quietly off the ATV and followed us to the entrance.

When we entered the corridor, Katia's dad started yelling in Creole, and got the response we were hoping for: a man guided us back through a dark hallway to a treatment room. The treatment room was small, about 8 feet × 10 feet, with three gurneys and a few empty shelves. Two frantic Haitian nurses barely looked up as we blasted into the room. There were two and three injured and bleeding patients on each gurney, lying side by side or crossways, sharing the small space allotted. We received no direction. I asked if the nurses spoke English, *"Parlez vous anglais?"* Their response was minimal at best. I continued to talk in a broken French and Creole mix, explaining that Katia was hurt and bleeding, that she needed attention immediately, and asked where we should take her. One nurse completely ignored our presence as she busily ran around trying to find the supplies that the other nurse was shouting out for into the air. The nurse who seemed to be in charge had gloves on, hemostat in one hand, suture material in the other; she pointed with her elbow to the end of the gurney by her current patient's feet. She was just starting to stitch up a head wound and was having difficulty controlling the bleeding, which was obscuring her view of the wound edges. David and I were very uncertain about what to do. I surveyed the room for supplies and noticed hardly any; no gowns, no gauze, no gloves. I thought to myself that this must not really be a treatment room, given the lack of intravenous set-ups and barren shelves. David thought the same, but said it out loud. He put Katia down on the gurney as directed by the nurse who seemed to be in charge. I took over the turban hold and the neck positioning for Katia while David went to see what was going on in the building.

Katia's dad was nowhere to be found. My hands were full, and David was determined to find help for Katia. I blew more mucus out of Katia's airway, forgetting that my hands were again importantly occupied with her head and her neck, and that I didn't have David's shirt to spit on and wipe off my mouth. I sputtered, directing the fluids onto my shirt away from Katia, wiping the drool onto my shoulder as best I could.

The large nurse at the head of the gurney continued to shout at the other nurse who kept circling the room, and then left the room, only to quickly come back empty-handed. David followed the empty-handed nurse back into the room in what seemed like an instant. He calmly reported that there were now many, many injured people flocking into the dark hallway, and that there was one doctor here at the hospital who was also already working on several patients at once. David found no other nurses or supplies. He gently wiped my face with the corner of his shirt. This situation was dire. Katia was not next in line.

David offered to hold Katia's head and neck, cocking his knee to extend the length of her support, keeping pressure on the wound and positioning her neck just right so she could breathe. I decided to help the charge nurse so we could get to Katia faster. My hands and clothes were covered with Katia's blood and secretions. I implored the frenetic smaller nurse to find me a gown and a pair of gloves, *"Si vous plais, si vous plais, si vous plais!!!* [Please, please, please!]" I said a quiet prayer. She came back a few minutes later with one gown and one pair of gloves. Thank you, Lord, for the little things.

There was no place to wash, so I donned the gown and gloves over dried blood and grime and offered my help to the nurse in charge. I understood her frustration in both the big situation of so many injured with so few supplies, and the small situation of not being able to see what she was trying so hard to repair. I blotted her patient's blood with some gauze the other nurse finally found, revealing the suture line she was trying to follow. We worked together and managed a good repair. She escorted the patient out of the room, and before David could move Katia onto the full gurney, she came back with another patient to take that briefly unoccupied spot. David and I exchanged glances of confusion as she started to work on this new patient who also had a full scalp injury. She said the doctor would come in to look at Katia. Katia's breathing was shallow and noisy again. I gave another strong breath. My hands were free, but I had gloves on with another patient's blood on them. There were no new gloves. I had mucus in my mouth. I spit and again used David's shirt.

The charge nurse was pouring betadine antiseptic directly into the large scalp wound, soap and blood mixing and cascading onto the floor; there were still no sponges to catch the fluids. I spotted a t-shirt on the gurney and uncomfortably decided to use it under the patient's neck to stabilize his position and soak up some of the fluids. I had already gotten past the lack of a new pair of gloves. I developed the mindset that I was just extremely grateful I *had* a pair of gloves. The nurse and I worked quickly together to remove as many scalp fragments and pieces of gravel as we could from the wound, then stitched up this patient's scalp while we awaited the doctor's arrival to assess Katia. As we knotted off the last suture, the charge nurse abruptly got up from her chair and began tending to another patient on the adjacent gurney two feet from us, again leaving us alone with Katia crosswise on the gurney. At this point, there was a lot of commotion outside in the hall, with yelling and crying and moaning. The doctor breezed in, removed Katia's father's t-shirt from her head, and directed me to suture her scalp wound and said, "No hope, too many others." He dropped some suture material on the gurney, along with a lone hemostat, and breezed out of the room as quickly as he had entered less than one minute earlier.

David and I exchanged tearful glances. Katia's cranium was exposed as she laid limp on the gurney, but she was breathing well and had a fairly strong pulse. She was unconscious and unresponsive, her deep tendon reflexes were nonexistent, and her pupils were dilated. She likely had a severe neck injury along with the head injury. She had been caught in the avalanche and she was not going to make it. We wanted to close up her scalp so she would stop bleeding and her father could hold her and say goodbye. I was now working on my third patient with the same pair of gloves and no gauze sponges, but I did have a quarter-full bottle of betadine antiseptic soap. Out of the corner of my eye, I noticed a large man occupying an entire gurney in the corner of the room, who had been unattended for the entire time we were in the treatment room. I saw that he also had an extensive scalp wound, along with many other lacerations elsewhere on his extremities. I decided to save the antiseptic for him.

I refocused on Katia, trying to find a syringe and lidocaine to numb her tissue before suturing. The one syringe I found broke as I drew up the lidocaine. There were no others. I continued to sew Katia together with no anesthesia. She was unresponsive to pain. I realized that I only had one package of suturing material, which would not be enough if I used up the length to knot and cut between each stitch. David helped me close up Katia's head, holding the retracted edges of her scalp. It had to be good enough. There was no other option. I had to adopt a "good enough" philosophy immediately, or I would have been frozen into uselessness.

What I didn't know was that during this hour or two, Willem had already dropped the elder woman from the village off at the hospital for care, staying just long enough to see that he needed to leave immediately and bring back both help from our team and supplies. Brian and one of my graduate students, Sara, along with a Haitian driver and his brother, went up to the clinic in the old dump truck, and packed the back of the truck with supplies: gauze, gloves, gowns, bandages, suturing material, hemostats, antiseptic soap and antibiotics, pain medication, syringes, IV solution, and tubing. Willem headed back to the hospital with a truck full of my teammates, and Brian followed close behind with a truck full of lifesaving supplies.

Because I did not know any of this was happening, I was completely surprised when a voice I recognized immediately came from the doorway, just as we were finishing with Katia. "Hey Sue! Can I help you?" I twisted around to see Stephan, coming into the treatment room. "Mr. Brian should be here soon with a whole truckload of supplies! He is bringing everything!" Stephan exclaimed. "My dad and I just got here with everyone from the team. They are taking care of everyone in the hallway. It's crazy out there—there are a lot of really badly hurt people out there. People crying and yelling, bones sticking out everywhere, blood all over," Stephan paused and said quietly, ". . . and some dead people." My heart sank to a new low. Stephan was composed and again asked if he could help me; could he translate for me?

My heart was now in my throat, thinking of 13-year-old Stephan, seeing and hearing this horror. Completely conflicted, with my hands still on Katia, I looked at dear Stephan and asked him if he thought he could find Katia's dad. Without hesitation he said he would try. Miraculously, he found both her dad and her mom. David and Katia's parents took Katia out of the treatment room, to where I did not know. Stephan stayed with me.

14 | THIRD HOUR: JOHN OLIVIER

By compassion we make others' misery our own, and so, by relieving them, we relieve ourselves also.
—THOMAS BROWNE, SR.

THE THIRD HOUR AFTER THE EARTHQUAKE, I QUICKLY SHIFTED MY THOUGHTS AND MY FULL ATTENTION TO THE LARGE MAN ON THE GURNEY IN THE CORNER, TO WHOM MY SHORT GLANCES HAD BEEN INTERMITTENTLY DARTING FOR THE PAST ONE OR TWO HOURS. HIS NAME WAS JOHN OLIVIER. I WAS ABLE TO ASCERTAIN WITH MY BROKEN CREOLE HIS NAME, HIS AGE OF 30 YEARS, AND THE FACT THAT HE WAS THE FATHER OF THREE YOUNG CHILDREN. I ALSO DEDUCED THAT HE WAS AN AMAZING PILLAR OF STRENGTH. HE WAS HUGE, WITH SHOULDERS TOO WIDE FOR THE THIN MATTRESS. THE CROWN OF HIS HEAD WAS FOUR INCHES OFF THE TOP OF THE GURNEY AND HIS FEET WERE AT LEAST A FOOT OFF THE GURNEY, WITH THE END OF THE TABLE REACHING ONLY TO MID-CALF. HE SEEMED TO BE BIONIC.

No wonder he wasn't able to share the old rolling bed with another patient. He had a giant scalp wound, literally from ear to ear, but he was no longer actively bleeding. It was as if someone had opened his scalp and put a bowlful of black-cherry Jell-O on top of his head; his blood had coagulated that dark a red. A low-toned but lively chat between Stephan and John Olivier ensued. I could understand a few words here and there, but I no longer had an ear for linguistics. I had focused my concentration on his injuries. I noticed several other large gashes, one on his elbow and another on his arm. The entire heel of his left foot was completely de-skinned, and the flayed skin was flapping from the meeting point of the arch of his foot to the end of his heel, as if the sole of his foot was the sole of a broken leather shoe. But of course, he had no shoes.

A noisy blend of shouting, crying, screaming, and moaning abruptly came in blasts each time the door opened. The sounds were no longer startling, but they remained extremely unnerving. I continually looked up to see who was coming in. As I was beginning to feel totally overwhelmed with John Olivier's head injury, the door opened, the noise entered, and the Haitian doctor/surgeon reappeared. *Oh, Lord, thank you!* In a 30-second consultation, the doctor told me to suture up John Olivier's peripheral wounds and then to bring him to the operating room, where the doctor would work on his scalp. He made reference to sewing up an older woman's face that had been ripped off, and then left the room as abruptly as he had come in.

David was back. As he searched the room for supplies, he enthusiastically reported that our team had already set up a triaging system. They were ripping up their scrubs and using the rags as bandages. They were splinting dangling, broken limbs with broken broomsticks and anything else straight and strong they could find in order to stabilize the injuries and decrease the agonizing pain. He contemplated a moment and then continued his report: the injuries were severe, like those a MASH (mobile army surgical hospital) unit would see. There were dozens and dozens of Haitians coming in droves, but Katia was in a hospital bed and her parents were sitting with her. The miniscule peace of mind I gained from knowing that Katia was comfortable with her parents by her side gave me the energy surge I needed to continue. I soothed myself further by thinking, *Thank God, Brian will be here soon with the supplies!*

As David talked, I cleaned John Olivier's wounds with the antiseptic I had saved specifically for him. The treatment room floor had been very slippery with all of the blood and betadine spills, but it was starting to dry. I strategically placed Katia's dad's blood-drenched t-shirt on the floor under the end of the gurney to catch the splashes as I poured the red soap into John Olivier's wounds. In the corner of the room, I spied a crumpled yellow paper gown, which looked free of stains and had pure white cotton cuffs, perfect for dabbing and drying John Olivier's wounds so I could begin his repairs. I had no functioning syringes or needles to use to inject the numbing medication into his skin before stitching him up. Prior to this moment, I had reluctantly but desperately compromised my deeply ingrained habits regarding sterile technique, universal protection, and precautionary measures. This, though, was where I drew the line: I would not reuse a needle. Stephan explained my position, and John Olivier smiled and stoically replied, "*Dacore, no pwoblem* [OK, no problem]."

I did make one last-ditch attempt at using a syringe, the same type I had tried to use before, which repeatedly and frustratingly broke each time I struggled to release the accumulated air in the syringe prior to an injection. I decided to experiment with this syringe by leaving the clean needle in the vial and squirting as much anesthesia as I could into the open wounds. That might help ease the pain of suturing just a bit. If it worked, I could continue to reuse the sterile syringe. However, if it didn't work, I would be in no worse a dilemma. It worked once, as I plunged a syringe full of anesthesia into John's heel. However, it did not work a second time. There was still chaos all around the treatment room, with the two Haitian nurses in the eye of the storm, paying no attention to me in the corner.

Stephan easily and naturally conversed with John Olivier, with the same thoughtful demeanor he had previously shown with

Richard, the young boy with the burnt face, earlier in the week. I started to sew together John Olivier's leather-like sole. John Olivier didn't flinch. He kept repeating, "*Merci, merci, Bondye beni ou! Dacore, no pwoblem* [Thank you, thank you, God bless you! It's OK, no problem!]." My stitching needles kept bending and breaking in his foot, leaving me no option but to retrieve the broken needle halves with my lone hemostat and repeatedly start over, making more attempts than I can recollect. Eventually, out of suture material, I was forced to pause. A frustrated gaze up to my mangled patient was met and returned to me with breath-stopping upturned lips and stunning white teeth. I moved nearer to his face and looked deeply into the warmth of his lovely brown eyes. As he patted my hand and I swiped at the tear making a slow descent down my cheek, I thought to myself, *What an amazing man! He truly is the face of God, the face of Haiti.* Under my feet I felt a strong tremor. After stilling myself completely for a moment, I questioned out loud, "Is the earthquake really not over? What is happening to Haiti?!"

Brian must have just arrived with the supplies. Sara, the last of my students, bounded into the treatment room with a stack of suturing materials, two willing gloved hands, and a heart held together by the tenacity of compassion. What an extremely welcome sight! Her synchronized work was skilled and filled with grace as she anticipated all of my needs. We were still lacking gauze sponges, and I was again desperate to find any remnant of something clean and dry to wipe the blood from John Olivier's laced-up wounds. As I repeated yet another survey of the room, I saw a flash of white on a gauze sponge, which must have been carelessly discarded or dropped to the floor. I summoned to Sara, as I pointed with my elbow and brushed away the hair falling into my face with my filthy forearm, "Do you see that bloody gauze sponge over there with the small patch of clean white? Can you grab it for me, please?" With a pathetic, questioning look, she did as I asked and put the desired sponge in my reaching fingers. After exchanging understanding looks between Sara and John Olivier, I took the used piece of cotton material and dabbed off the fresh blood

I had released while sewing up John Olivier's heel. He again reassured me with another smile of serenity and strength and repeated, *"Merci, merci, Bondye beni ou! Dacore, no pwoblem"*; this time he added, *"Mwen prie por ou."* I held his hand and responded, *"Mwen prie por ou, ausi, John Olivier, mon cherie* [I pray for you, too, John Oliver, my dear]."

I will not leave you or forsake you. These words floated into my busy thoughts as I simultaneously requested Stephan to find Brian in order to help David walk John Olivier to the operating room. It was finally time for his scalp repair.

Stephan found Brian moving back and forth throughout the chaos of the hall, another treatment room, the operating room, and the room that was being used as a sick ward. All areas were overflowing with severely injured people, some with loved ones supporting them to keep them up off the floor, others holding their own severed limbs together. People were wailing and screaming, children were sobbing, the sounds coming in waves of excruciating physical pain and emotional sorrow. The hall and the rooms were dark, with the exception of a few dimming singleton bulbs hanging precariously from the ceilings, powered by an unreliable generator, and a few headlamps on white faces from Chicago. Directives were being shouted out from all corners of the building.

Our team of 20 triaged the wounded, reluctantly sending away many families to carry a beloved family member home to die. The team worked together like a well-oiled machine, placing intravenous fluids, bracing and supportively wrapping open fractures, washing and suturing wounds after picking out stones and gravel, administering pain medication and antibiotics, and transporting the nonambulatory with the strength of their own backs and the escort of anyone who could help. Brian, Ray, James, and David, the men on our team, overhead-lifted and carried wounded from place to place either on a stretcher or an old door, through a sea of people, stepping over those too injured or weak (or dead) to move out of their way. The men were all moving fast and furious. When Stephan told Brian that I needed him, Brian came to me right away.

15 | FOURTH HOUR

*The world breaks everyone and afterwards
many are strong at the broken places.*
—ERNEST HEMINGWAY (1899)

THE MEN GOT JOHN OLIVIER INTO THE OPERATING ROOM. I FOLLOWED AFTER BRIAN, APOLOGETICALLY LEAVING SARA AND STEPHAN BEHIND IN THE TREATMENT ROOM.

THE DARK AND THE NOISE SEEMED UNCHANGED FROM THE SHORT BLASTS I HAD RECEIVED EACH TIME THE TREATMENT ROOM DOOR WAS OPENED. THE CHAOS, HOWEVER, SEEMED TO BE ESCALATING. MARY, OUR TEAM'S COORDINATOR, SAW ME IN BRIAN'S SHADOW HOLDING ONTO THE BACK OF HIS OVERALL STRAPS AND USING THEM AS MY GUIDE. SHE FOLLOWED ME INTO THE OPERATING ROOM. IN ORDER TO STAY FOCUSED, I DID NOT PERUSE THE CROWD; I PUT MY FOREHEAD INTO BRIAN'S BACK AND JUST KEPT WALKING AS HE WALKED. THE HAITIAN DOCTOR NEEDED AN ASSISTANT, WHOM HE HAD DETERMINED WOULD be me. Not only was Mary willing to be a gopher for the doctor and me, but having this time together to debrief would also prove to be a tremendous gift. She would definitely be able to fill in the gaps for me regarding the time I had been separated from the rest of the team. To be my eyes and ears where I am not: this had been her intuitive role in the clinic over our past several trips, which at this critical time continued to be her strength and her blessing.

In between instructions from the doctor and questions from me, Mary proudly spoke of the stalwart compassion of each of our team members, how they had spoken frankly to each other in the guest-house as they decided who would go to the hospital and who would not. During the drive up to the hospital in the back of the pickup truck, they attempted to emotionally prepare each other for the severe traumatic injuries and death they were expecting to witness. They reminded each other of the past week they had spent together in the rudimentary but well-supplied clinic in the mountains of Haiti, working day and night, side by side, in synchrony on the same physical, emotional, and spiritual planes. They reiterated how they knew that they were good for each other and good with each other, and that their unswerving desire was to help the Haitians and each other through whatever God put before them. They prompted each other to remember the prevailing theme of our trip: to see the face of God in all whom we saw, met, talked to, and touched; to make both physical and eye contact; to listen well and to care deeply. As we were tending to John Olivier and listening to each other, another prevailing thought took root in my mind: This situation of human horror was going to extend into the strengths of our camaraderie, compassion, skills, and faith. Our counter was to face the challenge set before us together and with conviction. Praise God, we were countering.

Mary continued to tell me details of the many patients in the other rooms. Dawn, a very seasoned, experienced nurse practitioner with whom I share a deep friendship, also updated me. Mary reassured me that the students were an absolutely amazing group of young woman, who were all "doing well." She also reluctantly confided that one of the team members had vomited and another had fainted, but told me that they were now both fine and they had definitely returned to treating patients. Maybe it was something they ate, maybe the heat, maybe the response to stress hormones being released by the bucketfuls.

John Olivier kept his eyes closed while we were closing up his scalp, but I don't think he was sleeping. I knew he wasn't dead. It appeared that the lidocaine used to numb the skin on his head was working, because he didn't flinch, even when we were close to his eyes. But then again, he was tougher than nails, like so many other Haitians I have had the pleasure to know. He was eerily still but breathing normally. I kept speaking to him to assess his neurological status: *"John Olivier, commo ca va?* [How are you?]." He continued his mantra-like response: *"Dacore, no pwoblem. Merci, merci, Bondye beni ou! Mwen prie por ou."* We started an intravenous line and planned to give him antibiotics. Brian came in to take him somewhere to recover, and I told him I would check in on him later.

Mary and I left the relatively quiet, almost peaceful operating room to brave the frenetic situation everywhere else. We each went in a different direction to see how the team was doing, to see where we could be of the greatest assistance. As I went from person to person, I started some IVs and helped to suture and bandage where I could be helpful, discovering that many patients who had been treated earlier had since gone home to recover. Their families carried them however they could, on chairs or pieces of scrap, or just supporting them as they walked together, taking with them antibiotics, analgesics, and clean bandages. Mary figured that in the past several hours our team had treated and sent home about 50 people. They also sent home several patients to die. They encountered several who were dead on arrival. There were at least another 50 people needing to be treated.

I observed my friends skillfully and desperately working together to save lives. But more amazing and important than that were the Haitian patients. I was privileged to bear witness to their endurance of an inexplicable level of suffering and anguish, tolerated with astonishing dignity, stoicism, and hope.

16 | FIFTH HOUR

We can do no great things,
only small things with great love.
—MOTHER TERESA

I SOUGHT OUT BRIAN SO I COULD FIND OUT WHERE JOHN OLIVIER WAS RECOVERING. BRIAN TOLD ME THAT THERE WERE NO RECOVERY BEDS. HE EXPLAINED THAT ALL OF THE BEDS IN THE HOSPITAL WERE CURRENTLY OCCUPIED BY PREVIOUSLY ILL PATIENTS WHO WERE ABLE TO PAY FOR THEIR CARE. THE ADMINISTRATOR OF THE HOSPITAL WAS UNCERTAIN HOW TO ALTER THIS DIFFICULT, CRITICAL, AND QUICKLY CHANGING SITUATION. BRIAN HAD HAD NO CHOICE BUT TO SIT JOHN OLIVIER IN A SMALL CHAIR AT A SMALL TABLE IN THE BREAK ROOM. HE WAS AT THE HOSPITAL BY HIMSELF. THERE WAS NO ONE TO TAKE HIM HOME. BRIAN REASSURED ME THAT HE WOULD CONTINUE TO CHECK ON JOHN OLIVIER AND AS SOON AS THE ADMINISTRATORS COULD FIGURE OUT A BETTER PLACE FOR HIM, BRIAN WOULD GET HIM SITUATED AND would let me know. I felt reassured and went to give more help to the others back in the treatment room. The barren shelves in the treatment room were now stocked with supplies brought by Willem, which just a few hours ago had been on the shelves of his mountain clinic. I was even more reassured.

When Brian went back to check on John Olivier, he found the large man slipping off the chair, with his legs sprawling and his head slumped on his folded arms on the table, quiet and still. Brian yelled to him in English, "Hey buddy, hey buddy. John Olivier, are you with me?" John Olivier picked up his head and smiled at Brian, giving him a thumbs-up, the universal sign for wellness. Brian went to the administrator and begged for a bed. Shortly thereafter, he came to me to take me to where John Olivier was resting. I again followed Brian holding onto his overall straps, but this time my head was upright and moving from side to side rather than tucked deep into the hollow of his back. There were still so many injured, so many who needed help. I am certain that I was traveling through the dull hall because the faces I saw were changing, but I wasn't aware of my arms and legs moving. The previously acute, sharp agony of screams and wails that my ears had endured were now muffled groans and sobs. As I continued to move through the corridor, surveying each room, I realized that my senses were starting to numb, which was a good thing at that moment in time. I also was numb to the seismic tremors that had been regularly occurring throughout the night.

Brian led the way to a considerably larger back room where I had not yet been. There were about 20 beds, 10 on each side, some with a rickety chair next to the bed, some with nothing next to the bed. All of the beds had patients lying on them; some mattresses were covered with very old linen, but most beds had no linen and no pillow. The bed frames were old, peeling, pitted metal, and the mattresses were equally old, stained and really gross. At least a few of the mattresses were plastic, which would be very warm and sticky in the humid heat of Haiti, but were at least more sanitary. The room was dingy and dark with minimal overhead lighting, powered by a generator, flickering but certainly not creating a soothing ambiance. I was actually grateful that the lighting was so poor. It became a conscious decision not to strain my eyesight in order to see all of the disgusting details regarding the condition of the hospital; I simply chose not to waste my night vision on the inhumane particulars of this place. Brian had given me a headlamp so I could direct the light beam to what I needed and chose to see clearly. The rest was best left in the dark.

John Olivier was all the way in the back of the room, in the corner, resting in what appeared to be a fairly comfortable state. He had gotten lucky, with a plastic mattress and some piece of clothing supporting his neck and head. As I was walking toward John Olivier, past the other beds in this turn-of-the-century hospital ward, I saw Katia in a bed, midway down the other side of the room. Her mom and dad were by her bedside, and they were holding her hands. As my steps took me steadily toward her bedside, I could hear her noisy, phlegmy breathing. A familiar expression from her dad's eyes locked into my eyes as he whispered to me, "*Madame, si vous plait, respire grand, encore, por tifi, mon cherie,*" asking me to help his sweet daughter breathe better again, like I did before. My internal voice responded, *Oh, no! I haven't had anything to eat or drink since breakfast. I just got the salty taste of her mucus out of my mouth a short while ago, and I have, up until now, been successful in keeping the bile that continues to rise in my esophagus from coming all the way up and out!*

Her dad continued to look at me pleadingly. I took a couple of my own deep breaths before producing a short, fast blow into her mouth. The mucus cleared and her breathing became quiet and gentle again. This time I was able to use my hands to lift up my scrub top and wipe my face and mouth onto my undershirt. There was mucus all over her face. They thanked me and wiped her face with an old t-shirt. Her dad was still not wearing a shirt. Katia was going to die. They should take her home away from this place. But it was too late, they lived a good distance away and the roads were difficult to travel in the dark. Here is where they were resigned to staying. They sat back next to Katia and patted her hands, stroked her arms, and kissed her forehead. I was glad I did not have a camera.

I redirected my focus to John Olivier as my feet took me to the corner of the room where he appeared to be comfortably resting on a sheetless plastic mattress, with his head on a naked pillow. My pocket held the bounty from our mountain clinic, which included several sterile, white gauze sponges; an alcohol pad; and a large, sterile hypodermic needle with a sterile, functioning syringe filled with lifesaving antibiotics, which I wanted him to receive immediately before he could die of sepsis. My freshly gloved hand rested softly on his arm as I told him that my big needle would pinch and sting a bit. He put his hand on my arm with a gentle reciprocal gesture and quietly uttered, *"Merci, merci, Bondye beni ou! Dacore, no pwoblem,"* and then once more added, *"Mwen prie por ou!"* I am certain that this amazing man was held together not by the too-many stitches-to-count treatment that we gave him, but by an inner tenacity and resilience I doubt I will ever personally know. What a privilege to have spent this time with John Olivier. I need no photograph to remember him.

17 | Sixth and Seventh Hours: Natalie

> *The best and most beautiful things in the world cannot be seen, heard or even touched. They must be felt with the heart.*
> —Helen Keller

Hours six and seven after the earthquake . . . many of the team members had not eaten since breakfast and had emptied their water bottles hours ago. They had been using their clean water to wash their hands, to quench the thirst of many injured, and to wipe sweaty and damaged brows. Thirst, hunger, and fatigue certainly were looming over each person on the team, even though the adrenaline rush of the evening was still masking their bodily exhaustion. Stressors such as physical threat, excitement, noise, bright lights, and high ambient temperature are the major physiologic triggers of adrenaline release. All of these stimuli are processed automatically in the central nervous system, without conscious deliberation. With uncontrolled surges of the fight-or-flight hormone during an intense stressor, such as during the earthquake and the hours following, the stomach and intestines stall and do not feel hungry, while at the same time blood glucose levels rise, thanks to the immediate response of the liver, providing energy to starving cells. The pupils become hyperreflexive to sharpen vision; the heart beats faster, circulating sugared-up blood to every corner of the reactive body; the lungs become more efficient, allowing the body to oxygenate at high speed despite an empty tank; and the brain can see, hear, and smell detail that surpasses typical observation. Intuition is keen.

I finally had a chance to walk throughout the hospital rooms to see how everyone on the team was doing. Most were working together in our buddy system, tag-teaming in response to each other's needs. They were engaged in a common sense—not in the meaning of a practical type of sense, but rather a kind of sixth sense that was intimately shared between the partners. They were interpreting the situation in unison, without verbal communication, while simultaneously anticipating the next essential supply, action required, or assistance needed. Reassurance to their patients and to each other was high, mostly through body language, which I've decided is the strongest form of communication. A lingering hand on a tense shoulder, the steady support of a quivering elbow, a firm hold of a broken leg elicit a more personal meaning than words, even when the words are spoken in a common dialect. An understanding, empathetic expression, accompanied by an intentional meeting of the eyes, completes the silent conversation by adding intonation to the unspoken words. This was what I had the honor of observing after so many hours of extreme trauma care in a sub-par facility. Americans were meeting Haitians in an extremely unusual situation and we would be bonded for life. It was powerful.

In a country where fuel is typically a scarce commodity, during a crisis of any kind—be it political or a natural disaster such as a hurricane—gasoline, diesel fuel, and propane gas are frequently protected by a uniformed or armed guard. The extent of the earth-quake throughout the city had not yet been realized, since all cellular communication throughout the island was disturbed and the Internet was spotty at best. The only functioning medium was satellite com-munication, and that too was inconsistent. But the intuition of the gas station owners, in the area of Port-au-Prince where we were located, was to bring the guards, armed with machine guns, out in full force to protect the pump stations and control who was and was not allowed fuel. During my rounds, I heard about the team's gas station stop dur-ing the truck ride up to the hospital seven hours earlier.

As Willem and the team headed back to the hospital, Willem knew he needed to get fuel before this precious resource was gone. There was already a full array of vehicles at the fuel station and a line down the road when the pickup approached the entrance to the sta-tion. There were several machine-gun-toting guards around the sta-tion, aggressively and loudly yelling at all of the would-be customers. Willem was in the cab of the truck, but the open back of the truck exposed 15 Americans crammed together, dressed in scrubs and wear-ing stethoscopes around their necks. All faces in the truck bed were as wide-eyed and open-mouthed as startled frogs.

The scene they were witnessing became less disconcerting as the uniformed, armed men went from pointing their machine guns at the truck to waving their machine guns from the truck toward the pumps. Within the few seconds it took to process the situation, the armed men switched to intimidating the scores of other queued vehicles, and directed the other drivers to maneuver their cars to allow our truck to proceed past them and toward the closest pump. The unanimous recounting of this moment was that the scores of vehicles coopera-tively parted like the Red Sea to allow our truck to pass. The guerillas called out directives to both Willem and the crowd, while pumping fuel into the pickup's tank. The atmosphere felt riotous, and everyone was relieved when the truck rolled out of the crowd and back onto the road leading up to the hospital. They were fortunate to have a full tank of diesel to get the team to the injured. Thank God for the international recognition of—and at this critical moment, respect for—scrubs and stethoscopes!

When the truck with the team arrived at the hospital, another mob-like situation was brewing. There were already more than 100 severely injured men, women, and children in the parking lot, along with their families, all attempting to gain entrance into the hospital, pushing and yelling, wailing and screaming. The team emptied from the truck a good distance from the entrance doors, forming a human chain by linking tightly to each other as they tried to create a path amongst the people. It was dark and they could barely make out the injuries of those closest to them. Once in the hallway, they had some scanty light, and their pupils were accommodating in a superhero night-vision manner, thanks to the recent adrenaline surges from both the earthquake and the situation at the gas station. They quickly put into motion their plan for triaging the wounded. Too soon into the triage process, they were put in the sad position of sending home some of the mortally mangled or dead with a loved one. But many others were quickly moved into treatment rooms or were cared for directly in the hall. The team was already aware of the lack of supplies, and was anticipating Brian's arrival with the dump truck any minute. Until the truckload of supplies arrived, they made do with cut-up scrubs for bandages and whatever they could find for splints.

As I continued my rounds, I learned that just a short while before, a few of the team members had gone back to the guesthouse, accompanying Stephan. They were not feeling well. One had fainted, another vomited, one needed medication, and Stephan needed some buddies. The situation had become overwhelming, too much for an adult, let alone a 13-year-old. I was glad to hear that our team was taking care of each other along with the injured. The thick bonds of their camaraderie could not have been cut with even the sharpest of knives.

I finally made it over to the corner of the other treatment room and saw the back of Natalie, a young woman sitting in a wheelchair, moaning rhythmically with every exhalation. She was sitting upright, but her neck was cocked back and every couple of seconds she would snap her head forward and groan loudly. Both hands were tightly grasping the arms of the wheelchair. The rest of her body was fairly still. As I walked toward her, I caught her eye when her head was in the backward position, just before she snapped it forward. When I got closer, I could see why she was in such misery: Her right leg was almost completely severed mid-thigh, with her broken femur in complete view. The two jagged, snapped ends of her femur were about six or eight inches apart, looking like a white branch broken in half after a terrible storm. The entire weight of the lower part of her leg was dangling from the seat of the chair, being held off the floor by some flesh and what was left of the backside of her thigh muscle. The lower part of her left leg was in the same gruesome condition, only it was her tibia that was detached and dangling.

"Oh my, oh my dear Lord, please help this woman. Please help me so I can help this woman. How is she alive?" I muttered to myself.

My teammates and I made tourniquets on the distal ends of the viable proximal limbs, but didn't know what to do with the dangling portions. These severed parts of the legs were not bleeding anymore and we knew that they would have to be removed. The Haitian doctor/surgeon was caring for patients as we brought the casualties to him. Natalie would have to be next. She also needed an intravenous line before she went into shock from fluid loss. Together, we rapidly wrapped and supported her legs so the weight of the hanging limbs was relieved. I had hoped that this dressing and some good painkiller would bring her a little relief, but I think the only relief was ours, in that her horrific injuries were no longer in plain view.

18 | EIGHTH HOUR: BRIAN

> *Do not allow yourselves to be disheartened by any failure as long as you have done your best.*
> —MOTHER TERESA

BRIAN WATCHES OVER ALL OF US WHEN WE ARE IN HAITI. HE IS STRONG, INTELLIGENT, OBSERVANT, LOGICAL, COMPASSIONATE AND EMPATHETIC, PATIENT, SELFLESS, TIRELESS, AND FAITHFUL. THESE CHARACTERISTICS ARE HIS NATURAL ATTRIBUTES, WHICH MEANS THAT HE DIDN'T HAVE TO TAKE TRAINING CLASSES TO LEARN HOW TO BE AN EFFECTIVE LEADER. HE IS FAIRLY SOFT-SPOKEN AND EASYGOING, BUT WHEN SOMETHING NEEDS TO BE SAID OR DONE, HE WILL USE HIS FULL VOICE (WHICH CAN BE QUITE LOUD) AND WHOLE SELF (WHICH CAN BE IMPOSING) AS NEEDED. I, IN CONTRAST, HAVE MY PHYSICAL LIMITATIONS, HAVE ONLY A FOCUSED INTELLECT, CAN BE VERY MYOPIC, "SPACEY," AND IMPATIENT, AND CAN BECOME SELF-ABSORBED IN A PROJECT TO THE POINT OF LOSING MY ENVIRONMENTAL AWARENESS. I AM an extrovert, but my voice is not very loud. Brian's and my innate characteristics mesh when it comes to compassion, empathy, energy, and faith. To summarize, we are mostly opposites with the exception of our heart personalities. I take on most of the outward leadership responsibilities for our Haiti teams, by organizing, instructing, guiding, and mentoring. However, Brian is the one that all of the team members' parents, spouses, girlfriends or boyfriends, and family want as their loved one's leader in Haiti.

That being said, I was extremely intent on establishing an intravenous line in Natalie's veins. I was *not* going to let her suffer any more and die of shock or sepsis just because we were unable to replace the fluids that she had lost or failed to give her antibiotics. She seemed more comfortable when her leg was supported and no longer hanging. We just needed to give her consistent pain medication, antibiotics, and fluids. Eventually, her leg would have to be cut off, before the severed part (75 percent of her leg) started to decompose. After all her agony and patience, I wanted her to make it to surgery, sometime in the next few hours. Hours? Days? I had become focused and attached—myopic. Natalie's veins were elusive because of her blood loss, but she was sitting upright, talking and occasionally yelling. When I found a vein worth attempting on her right hand, I carefully guided the needle and catheter into the vein and got a reassuring flash of blood. However, the fragile vein blew as soon as I attached the intravenous fluid, causing her hand around the vein to swell. I wanted to yell!

Several hours after our team arrived at the hospital, a young medical student, affiliated with the hospital, joined us. He was enthralled with Natalie's condition, inappropriately questioning how she could still be alive and still be so feisty, while at the same time wondering about the pathophysiology of phantom limb pain. "What's the pain like when the majority of a limb is severed, but the fleshy part of the leg is still attached?" he absurdly asked. I told him that the pain was bad, real bad, just look at poor Natalie! He was sizing up veins on her left hand and arm, poking at them with no organization, blowing several very viable vessels. Even though my first attempt was also not successful, I was being critically careful, scrutinizing each option for success.

I felt a rising annoyance with this student whom I did not know. He seemed to be attempting veins hurriedly, with a skill level that seemed quite low and an exuberance that felt like he was trophy-seeking. I didn't want him to blow one more vein! I wanted all the veins for myself. My face was flushing as I summoned strength to command him to stop. Just then, the building started shaking, the dull overhead lights went out, and the loud rumblings of the shifting ground mixed with screams. The medical student jumped up cussing and ran out of the room. I was happy! I now had both of Natalie's arms and all of her veins to myself. She would get her IV. Just then, Brian appeared at my side, I thought to help me. He grabbed my arm and yelled, "Mags, come on, COME ON! We have to leave. This is another big quake, and this building is not stable. We have to be done here. Everyone on the team is exhausted, and we need to get them home. It is dangerous here on the edge of this broken mountain. We have to go. It's way past midnight. Everyone else is in the truck, waiting for you. Don't make me carry you out!"

Brian lifted me up to my feet by my elbows, grabbed my hand, and darted down the dark, eerily quiet and almost empty hall, effort-lessly lifting me into the bed of the truck, where the rest of the team was waiting. The truck was idling; Brian lifted me into the truck and had barely closed the tailgate before Willem sped away. I was facing backward and saw the hospital still standing, but quickly leaving my view as we descended the mountain, with our headlights beaming into the midnight rock. Brian turned off my headlamp. The air was cool, damp, and quiet. No one was talking, which was a stark contrast from the hot, babbling chaos in the hospital. There was no reason or even ability to speak. Our minds were racing, our heads were reeling, and not one of us was yet able to let go of any thought that tried to sneak away into the dark. No matter how small, at this moment, each little detail was a keeper. I was unresolved, and would be for a very long time. The film in my memory was developing. I would need no digital enhancement to keep this photo album vivid.

Eight hours: the routine length of time for a normal workday shift, typically constituting an unremarkable blip of time from a day or a life. The past eight hours had been a shift none of us could ever have imagined. Every second and minute of those first eight hours will forever be remarkable and will always be hard to explain to others and to ourselves. The calm quiet of the truck in the night was a respite.

19 | AFTER THE EIGHTH HOUR

> *The future depends on what*
> *we do in the present.*
> —MAHATMA GANDHI

WE PULLED INTO A DARK DRIVEWAY THAT I DIDN'T RECOGNIZE. WILLEM LUMBERED OUT OF THE CAB TO THE BACK OF THE PICKUP WHILE MUMBLING A QUESTION TO ME, ASKING IF I WOULD TAKE A LOOK AT HIS FRIEND WHO HAD A HEAD INJURY. IT WAS NOT HARD TO HEAR HIS LOW VOICE. EVERYONE IN THE TRUCK BED WAS PIN-DROP QUIET. THE NIGHT WAS VERY STILL. IN THE DARK, I WAS HANDED A SMALL TRAUMA BAG SOMEONE HAD PREVIOUSLY PREPARED, AS SARA (WHO SILENTLY VOLUNTEERED TO HELP) AND I FOLLOWED WILLEM INTO THE HOUSE. AS WE ENTERED THE HOUSE, A WHITE WOMAN WHO HAD A TWO-INCH GASH IN HER HEAD, WHICH WAS NO LONGER BLEEDING, GREETED US. SHE OFFERED US SOMETHING TO DRINK. AT THIS POINT, I WAS REALLY thirsty but afraid to drink, as my bladder was asleep, and I didn't want it to wake up just yet.

With my current warped perspective, the woman's head injury and her other scrapes and bruises, even a likely broken arm, seemed miniscule. The laceration was in her scalp at the crown of her head, surrounded by lots of hair, and it was going to take me an hour to clean it, trim the hair, remove the debris, and then sew the fleshy edges together. It was so late! Everyone in the truck was exhausted. I was starting to feel a kind of mesmerized buzz, which happens as the stress response of adrenaline surges begins to recede, even as it continues to circulate. As I was picking the gravel out of the woman's wound, Sara gave her an antibiotic injection. We had no more tetanus. As Sara was preparing the other supplies, relief overcame me when Willem asked me if it would be ok to stitch the cut up later. "Yes! Definitely OK! Good for another eight to twelve hours for someone to stitch," I blurted. We made the decision together to leave the suturing, and the possible arm setting, until the next day.

The woman was grateful and kind and understanding of our "long night and fatigue," and said she would go to the hospital for treatment in the morning. I thought I responded, "OH NO! That's a really bad idea. That hospital is absolutely HORRIBLE! Just come by Willem's house first thing tomorrow and I will be happy to finish up the stitching before we leave for the airport." But I'm grateful that, in reality, my mouth was really tired and my lips did not open. I just followed Willem out the door.

Within another 15 minutes, we were back at the guesthouse. It was around 2:00 A.M. Beth, Willem's beautiful and gracious wife, shared with us that while she was alone in the house, she could hear singing coming from the mountains, concluding that the villagers must have gathered together at the church to soothe each other and lift their voices up to God in the dark of the night. Beth also considerately prepared some light food for us, not knowing if we would be ravenously hungry, or nauseated and unable to eat. We were a combination of both. After sitting at the table together, some chose to wash up and just go to bed, while others finalized their packing. We were scheduled to leave for the airport at 8:00 A.M., and the prevailing thought was that we were headed back to Chicago as planned.

Beth had gained some insight regarding the extent of the earthquake and had learned that it was quite a significant one: 7.0 on the Richter scale. She had received many calls while we were gone via their satellite phone, one of which was from a stateside reporter requesting an interview with us as soon as we returned from our trauma care at the hospital. She explained that everyone in the States wanted to know what the earthquake was like and what the conditions were like here. She feared that if we didn't share some information, he and the others would not stop calling. The availability of and basic ability for communication throughout the country had been inconsistent all evening, and firsthand information was scarce. Beth, Willem, and I thought it best to write a statement together to send to the Tribune reporter, which he could share with the others.

EMAIL: WEDNESDAY, JANUARY 13, 2010, 2:56 A.M.

Subject: Message for the Tribune

Will—

Our Little by Little team has been in Haiti working with Mountain Top Ministries (MTM) in the village of Gramothe, outside of Thomassin, about 15 km from Pétionville. We returned around 1:00 A.M. from a local hospital 5 miles further up the mountain, providing trauma care to at least 100 severely injured people, working with one Haitian physician, a few nurses, and a few other volunteers in conditions that were extremely poorly equipped to handle day-to-day care, let alone an emergency such as this.

We cut up scrubs to use for bandages, and used broom handles for splints, and used anything else we could find to stop bleeding—we have been there since 4:30 P.M. this afternoon. Supplies were brought to the hospital from the clinic at MTM, so we were then able to better provide for the sick/injured patients.

Many of our team members were walking home from a full day of clinic, down the mountain, crossing the riverbed, when the ground started shaking, causing many to lose their balance or to fall. The rocks tumbled from the sides of the mountain like an avalanche into the riverbed. Our team was safe, but many villagers got caught in the shifting, falling rocks, walls, and houses. Other members of our team who were back at the house also felt the quake with very strong tremors, causing the trees and the house to violently shake, but there was no collapse. Several brick walls and houses have tumbled where we are at in Thomassin and Gramothe; many, many severely injured. Communication throughout PAP is down, but we have been able to use email.

Thanks for reporting this catastrophe. The needs in Haiti are great!

Sue

PART THREE

AFTER THE EARTHQUAKE

20 | First Day After

Time is but the shadow of the world upon the background of eternity.
—Jerome K. Jerome

Willem returned from his trek down the mountain completely stunned at the total devastation he witnessed as he passed through the urban areas of Delmas and Pétionville. It appeared to him that nearly all of the buildings and dwellings had collapsed. There were injured people everywhere, with many other dead and injured stuck in collapsed buildings. The situation was so bad and so extremely chaotic that he couldn't continue traveling on the road further down into Port-au-Prince. Willem's head hung low as he softly acknowledged that he could do nothing right then for anyone he passed, so he turned around and came home. He thanked us for helping so many at the hospital last night, and for continuing to help again in his front yard today. There had not been an earthquake in Haiti in more than 200 years. No one knew what an earthquake was, what to do now, or what to do next. His country was suffering in a way it had never suffered before. He seemed despondent but not defeated.

He also learned that Katia had died during the night, and he had been asked to preside over her funeral. We were all invited to her funeral. I had mixed feelings about attending Katia's service. In fact, I was having another flashback.

Just six years earlier, I was enjoying some early morning gardening, tossing weeds and picking lily-of-the-valley for a bouquet. Brian and I had a houseful of guests, and they would soon all wake up and come to the kitchen. I wanted a "good morning" greeting of sweet, fresh flowers on the kitchen table. It was mid-May and my older son, Brad, was home for the summer after attending school in upper Michigan. My daughter, Maggie, had just gotten home from California following a successful first year at college. My youngest son, Kyle, was still living at home, excited to wrap up his junior year in high school and ready for summer to begin. My sister-in-law and her fiancé were in town for our niece's christening later that morning, and were planning on staying with us for the weekend.

It was eight in the morning when two uniformed policemen, accompanied by one professionally dressed woman, walked slowly but intently up my driveway, approaching me closely while asking my name and showing me their badges. I responded with my name, and they further questioned if anyone else was home, specifically asking if I was married and if my husband was home. As I remained squatting, silently perched on my toes among the flowers in my front garden, my husband, Brian, joined us. The officers requested that we go inside. They made hand motions directing us to the front door of the house and then to sit down while at the same time inquiring if we had a son named Bradley Edward Walsh. My legs were not moving, I couldn't speak, my lips were frozen, and my heart was pounding so loudly I couldn't even hear. I saw their lips moving in slow motion and their hands pointing to the front door, then to the chairs at the kitchen table.

I thought to myself, *How did I get from my garden to inside this kitchen I don't even recognize? Who are these people and what are they doing here? I can smell the sweet fragrance of the lilies-of-the-valley but I can't breathe. My heart has jumped out of my chest and is in my throat. I'm going to vomit and my heart is going to spill onto the floor.* Following the police instructions, Brian took my hand and pulled me into his lap as he sank into a chair. He was able to choke out, "Yes, we have a son named Brad." The three officers positioned themselves at the unfamiliar kitchen table and finished what they had come to tell us: Our son Brad had been in an accident. He was dead.

I looked at Brian, still not able to breathe or hear or recognize where I was, but I absolutely realized that my head was exploding. I was having a stroke. It made perfect sense. I couldn't move, I couldn't hear or see, my hands were going numb, my mouth was open, and even though I couldn't breathe I knew I was screaming. I could feel that my throat was on fire. Was my heart stuck in my throat, or did I vomit it out? What were these people saying? Brian was patting my head. Was my head still attached to my neck? I couldn't tell. Everyone in the house was now awake and came into the kitchen. I could see again, and I could see that Brad wasn't in the kitchen. Where was Brad? I was trying to yell, "Someone please go get Brad! He is a heavy sleeper! He was out late last night but now his truck is home! He left earlier in the evening in his truck and now it's obvious that his truck is in the driveway so he must just be sleeping and he's really hard to wake up. He needs to know that I've lost my mind, which is in my head, which is rolling around on the kitchen floor next to my heart!" But no words came out. I could feel my chest heaving and sobs floating up and out of my paralyzed mouth.

21 | FIRST NIGHT AFTER

In the same way, the Spirit helps us in our weakness.
We do not know what we ought to pray for,
but the Spirit himself intercedes for us with groans
that words cannot express.
—ROMANS 8:26

THROUGHOUT THE DAY, MARY HAD FIELDED A
NUMBER OF INCOMING CALLS FROM HER HUSBAND,
KEVIN, WHO, TOGETHER WITH SEVERAL PEOPLE FROM
HOME, WERE ASSESSING OUR SITUATION IN HAITI.
SHE ALSO SPOKE WITH A FEW REPORTERS WHO HAD
SOMEHOW GOTTEN HOLD OF OUR INCOMING SATEL-
LITE NUMBER AND WANTED MORE AND MORE INFOR-
MATION. ANNETTE, DAVID'S WIFE AND MY DEAR FRIEND,
WHO IS A SOCIAL WORKER, INTUITIVELY HAD HER FIN-
GER ON THE TEAM'S PSYCHIC PULSE. EVERYONE WAS
IN SHOCK AND DEALING WITH THE STRESS OF THE
LAST 24 HOURS DIFFERENTLY. WE WERE ALL ACUTELY
AWARE THAT NONE OF US KNEW EXACTLY HOW BEST
TO GET OURSELVES THROUGH EACH ADVANCING HOUR,
SO WE INDIVIDUALLY ALLOWED THE TIME TO PASS
BY DOING SOMETHING THAT FELT COMFORTABLE TO

ourselves—or rather, rolled into an activity that felt the least daunting. Most of the medical team became involved in the yard clinic in some way throughout the day; some worked for a bit and then took a break, others worked all through the light of day. Most of the non-medical team did not linger for any length of time in the yard. They diverted each other while being supportive and empathetic. They each knew what the bottom line was for the others' thoughts, and at that point there was no need for deep conversation. We were already getting advice from home that it would be a good idea to immediately conduct a debriefing session run by professionals trained in post-traumatic stress disorder. Some good friends were organizing such a session in Chicago, ready to mobilize us and initiate the treatment as soon as we arrived back in the States.

We gathered as we normally would for dinner, holding hands and saying grace. A nice meal had been prepared for us. Some of the team regained their robust appetites after missing several previous meals; others' gastrointestinal tracts were still slow to recoup. Either way, we were all sitting together in the dining room, attempting to relax. It had been an unreal 24 hours since the violent rumblings and devastation caused by the dramatic shifting of the Haitian earth.

More details about the earthquake were becoming accessible to us via the Internet and through our families via satellite phone; these details became the main topics of our dinner conversation. The more we learned, the more we realized how less than one minute of time could be so devastating to so many, and the greater our disbelief became. The 2010 Haiti earthquake (in Haitian Creole, *Tranblemanntè 2010 nan peyi Ayiti*) was a catastrophic magnitude 7.0 earthquake, with an epicenter near the town of Léogâne, approximately 25 km (16 miles) west of Port-au-Prince, Haiti's capital. We were closer to the epicenter than the worst-hit area of Port-au-Prince. No wonder the magnitude of what we felt and the damage we saw was so dramatic.

The United States Geological Survey recorded eight aftershocks in the two hours after the main earthquake, with magnitudes between 4.3 and 5.9. Within the first nine hours, 32 aftershocks of magnitude

4.2 or greater were recorded, and 12 of them measured magnitude 5.0 or greater. We had felt and been startled by each aftershock, but I don't think any of us were counting. I do know that some of us experienced repeated adrenaline surges with each renascent tremor.

The metropolitan area of Port-au-Prince is laid out like an amphitheater. The harbor and seaport, airport, major municipalities, commercial and landmark buildings are positioned as if at center stage. The residential regions fan up and wide into the surrounding foothills, creating a bowl-like effect around the center stage of these historic and utilitarian constructs. Estimating the number of people living in this heavily populated area is difficult, and I have seen numbers ranging from 2.5 to 3.5 million people. From these estimates, we know that more than one-third of the nation's total population of 9 million lives in an area of approximately 15 square miles. Amongst the widespread devastation and damage throughout Port-au-Prince and elsewhere, the vital infrastructure that was necessary to respond to the disaster was severely damaged or destroyed. The infrastructure casualties included all hospitals in the capital, the airport, the seaport, land transport facilities, and communication systems.

The earthquake caused major damage in Port-au-Prince and other settlements in the region, leaving many dead and trapping many others. Multiple notable landmark buildings were significantly damaged or destroyed, including the Presidential Palace, the National Assembly building, the Port-au-Prince Cathedral, and the Prison Civile de Port-au-Prince (the main jail); damage to the latter allowed approximately 4,000 inmates to escape. Many government and public buildings were also damaged or destroyed, including the Supreme Court, the Palace of Justice, and the headquarters of the United Nations Stabilization Mission in Haiti (MINUSTAH), and many in these buildings were killed. The quake affected the three Médecins Sans Frontières (Doctors without Borders) medical facilities around Port-au-Prince, causing one to collapse completely. A hospital in Pétionville also collapsed, as did the St. Michel District Hospital in the southern town of Jacmel, which was the largest referral hospital in southeast

Haiti. President René Préval and his wife Elisabeth Delatour Préval escaped injury.

The number of fatalities was not known at that time, but the death toll from an earthquake of such magnitude, occurring in such a densely populated area with such a weak infrastructure, was estimated to be in the hundreds of thousands. I can state that knowing all of these facts at that time became overwhelming and impossible to comprehend. Two things were clear: we were not exiting the country tomorrow, and we were fortunate to be staying with our friends.

As we were counting our blessings that first night after, another very large aftershock took hold, rattling and shaking the house and our insides. Again, we leapt to our already moving feet and were outside before the rumbling stopped. The structure of the house once again proved itself to be strong, and after a few minutes we were back in our chairs, finishing our meals, trying to settle our pounding hearts and frazzled nerves. No wonder the majority of Haitians planned to sleep outside! Everyone in Haiti was frightened that the next aftershock would be the one to collapse the roof over their heads. No one near Port-au-Prince had slept the night before, and there would be no rest for many who slept indoors that night either. Just as our vital signs recovered to near baseline, all six dogs in the yard began barking in a ballistic way, again setting off our "startle" buttons. Admittedly, we were jumpy and on edge. We were, however, pleasantly surprised to discover that the dogs' agitation was caused by 13 children from the orphanage, who were standing at the front gate, hoping to gain entrance into the yard. Even though the orphanage was not damaged during the earthquake, the children and their nannies became very frightened during the repeated aftershocks, and walked several miles in the dark to Willem's and Beth's home seeking comfort and reassurance. The worried expressions on the faces of the precious orphans melted into relief as we opened the gates, and they piled inside. Giggles and Creole squeals replaced the previously tense air. Pillows and blankets, towels, nightshirts, and snacks were found. Games were played. We had a slumber party!

22 | THE FOLLOWING DAYS

You must be the change you wish to see in the world.
—MAHATMA GANDHI

WILLEM WAS DRESSED IN PRESSED SLACKS, FORMAL SHIRT, AND TIE, AND WAS ALREADY PACING DOWN AND UP THE MOUNTAIN ROAD TO THE VILLAGE CHURCH BEFORE WE COULD EVEN CHECK OUR WATCHES. IT WAS THREE O'CLOCK IN THE AFTERNOON, AND WILLEM WAS HEADED TO KATIA'S FUNERAL. OUR MAKESHIFT YARD CLINIC WAS STILL FULL OF PATIENTS IN NEED. THERE WERE MANY STILL WAITING FOR TREATMENT, AND IT WOULD BE DARK IN LESS THAN TWO HOURS. NONE OF US WANTED TO LEAVE ANY PERSON UNTENDED. RATHER THAN GOING INTO THE VILLAGE, WE DECIDED TOGETHER TO STAY AT THE GUESTHOUSE TO BE SURE EVERYONE GOT CARE. MY NECK, WHICH WAS STARTING TO DETACH FROM MY HEAD AT THE THOUGHT OF GOING TO KATIA'S funeral, became stiff and strong, as we together finished up the afternoon in the yard.

Praise songs, from the voices of friends and family of Katia (the entire village), were as sweet as a lily as they floated from the adjacent mountain, finding our eager ears. Dusk came upon us, the yard was empty, and we moved into the guesthouse. There were messages to read from Chicago. We needed to reconvene and have a meeting.

EMAIL: THURSDAY, JANUARY 14, 2010, 9:39 A.M.

From: Maggie Walsh

Subject: Hi everyone

I just got off the phone with my dad. The phones are back up after being dead yesterday, but of course they have limited access to the phone and Internet, so I'm relaying his message to the best of my ability. :) They are all still safe and hanging in there, despite the tremors and aftershocks, one yesterday that, as a tremor, registered 6.0!

He said that they might be able to leave today, as they've heard that the airport will be open for private jets that fly in with aid. It sounds like they will be able to head back to Miami on one of these jets from a generous private construction company, I believe, in shifts of 11 people. Surely some of the details may change, but they are in contact with the right people and are hopeful that they will be able to get back stateside either tonight or tomorrow. They spent yesterday back up at the clinic and will likely be back today as well, making use of the time that they are there to be of help where they are needed.

Of course they, and I, are so thankful for your prayers and support. I will let you know if I hear anything else.

Maggie

EMAIL: THURSDAY,
JANUARY 14, 2010, 10:54 A.M.

From: Sue Walsh
Subject: We are fine

This is from Brian and Sue Walsh and the entire Chicago team in Haiti. Please forward to anyone we have missed. Thank you!

Just quickly while I have Internet access I want to clarify Maggie's email: we are totally fine, we are safe, we have food and water, and we have peaceful mountains and brilliant sun! We are all packed and will be ready to go whenever either the commercial planes (AA) are available or when any other option may be available. The route to the airport is safe and clear and all the Haitians everywhere are so appreciative of the help the rescue teams (which we are identified as) are providing.

The humanitarian aid is so important, so essential and certainly a priority. We are on Haitian time, which means being calm and patient with no clock-watching or any particular, certain agenda . . . .

Just keep the injured and those in need in your prayers, and be reassured by this email that we are well. We are so absolutely blessed to have such loving and well-connected family and friends at home, all working together to first get help here to the Haitians, but at the same time bring us back home to all of you. We do love you all so, and feel uplifted by all your prayers.

Sue and Brian

We continued to fill our time with our front-yard clinic, caring for those who were injured, passing out appropriate antibiotics and pain relievers as we received additional information about the horrors that engulfed Haiti. The real-time images from the varying media venues were of a ravaged and war-torn Caribbean country, struck quickly and ferociously by its elusive enemy, Mother Earth. Hundreds to thousands were already known to be dead. So many had died that the morgues were immediately full; identification of the mass number of dead bodies was impossible, so the dead were put in dumpsters, or simply piled in the streets, where they were already rotting from the brutal Haitian heat. So many had died that the survivors had resorted to burning corpses or burying them in mass graves—but only if a dump truck could find a path to where there was an accumulation of bodies, and then maneuver a passable road back to the grave sites.

Many others were still alive but buried in the debris. Countless numbers of people sent see-sawing calls through the fallen buildings, bending ears to recognize familiar voices, both sides of the rubble praying that rescue could be a possibility.

Personal and political empathy levels from around the world sky-rocketed. Medical and rescue teams from all able countries were quickly mobilized and poised for flight. Foreign aid was swiftly pledged in an unprecedented small number of hours. The media barrage brought the distraught Haitian mother, frantic father, horrified child, mangled fellow human being into audiences' homes and lives, magnetizing viewers to their screens, and compelling the watchers to dial in a donation. The observers could almost smell the dust and the putrid air; taste the salty tears mixed with blood and pain; feel the parched mouths, dried lips, and pure agony from the moving images and still photographs launched from digital sources in all the rooms of their houses. The dramatic sights and sounds were mobilizing worldwide response. It seemed the world was shaken and was wearing their hearts for Haiti on their sleeves. Yet, Haiti was too broken to handle the response.

I felt the dichotomy of this disaster very personally. Although I was residing within the most broken area of the country, I and my team were alive and unharmed. We had medical supplies, food staples, water, and were assisting our neighbors in any way possible; however, only a short distance away, there was an extreme lack of supplies for millions. The media barrage presented scenes that were nearly incomprehensible, and disturbing to the point of both daytime and nighttime nightmares, but even we—who were already in Haiti and wanted to do more—could not reach the many in need. Communication, transportation, municipalities, government, United Nations:

all systems were abruptly shattered. Our team was also immobilized by this broken country and could only help in the mountain village in our immediate vicinity.

Criticisms of inadequate and untimely action from the Haitian government were already appearing in sound bites and in print. It felt like the media were blaming Haiti for its inability to respond to overtures and offers of immediate help. These criticisms felt very wrong. The inability to give more help was more awful than anything we had previously experienced.

Emotions around the world were heightened, but logical thinking appeared to be displaced by misplaced and misconstrued empathy. The airport was critically damaged during the earthquake, rendering the control tower inoperable. Without air control, certainly no one could expect foreign flights, carrying supplies and aid workers, to be able to land safely. The seaport was also badly damaged, which meant that ships could not dock, and that smaller vessels could not immediately transport people or cargo in and out of the harbor. Because of the full collapse of ground transportation, due to obstructions of strewn heavy rubble, dead bodies, multiple injured, and milling people all in the streets, Port-au-Prince was stalled, in a dead standstill that was impossible to watch but equally impossible to alter, especially at the speed everyone was demanding.

The leadership of the country was in total and complete disarray. Haiti's president's life was spared, but the buildings in Haiti that are the equivalents of the U.S. White House, Pentagon, congressional quarters, and municipal structures, were all collapsed in Port-au-Prince, and many of Haiti's other leading officials lay dead under the rubble of the fallen essential buildings. A large number of the city's police force, other municipal workers, and the United Nations's International Guard forces were also killed as their government and international structures were demolished by the quake. Making the situation even more chaotic, a major prison cracked open, releasing approximately 4,000 prisoners into the reeling area of Port-au-Prince.

This entire disaster was one of unprecedented proportions. Préval was left to lead with few domestic resources or options for doing so. It should be noted that Haiti fought hard for its independence from slavery 200 years ago, and that foreign countries, in both the distant and recent past, have not always had Haiti's best interest in mind. It was entirely unrealistic for Préval, who was in essence without advisors, to be expected to manage this onslaught of information and render snap decisions on matters of such extreme importance; these decisions would affect not only the immediate well-being of his people, but also have profound, long-lasting ramifications in world politics. Pulling together a country fractured by the earthquake would be daunting for any leader, let alone a disarmed leader whose country had lacked structural, social, medical, educational, and political infrastructure prior to this natural disaster. I was now praying very hard for Préval.

Coinciding with Préval's mounting decisions were our own considerations for the safety and eventual evacuation of our team. How long would we have food and water, fuel and safety? There seemed to be enough dried and canned foods for a few more days, but there were 23 of us, 4 in our host family, and 13 orphans. Fresh items and bottled water would soon have to be purchased. The local grocery store had supplies, and Willem, having successfully secured diesel for his vehicles and holding tanks at the compound, would be able to get back and forth from the store. He had only a modest amount of cash, but even that small amount was a blessing, as the banks were also considerably damaged and were not functioning at this time. We had regular communication to the States and our loved ones via satellite by phone and Internet. We realized that the airport, seaport, and ground transport down to the city and throughout the city were nonexistent. We were getting more accustomed to the aftershocks, although they were always associated with a surge of adrenaline that triggered memory and emotion. We would have to wait for decisions to be made and actions to be taken. Our safety did not appear jeopardized while we remained in the protected calm of the mountains.

If we were going to continue to be productive in our yard clinic, we would need more supplies. Brian mentioned to us that the village clinic, although it appeared structurally sound, was in a shambles. Everything had been shaken off the shelves by the earthquake; he and Sarah had seen the damage when they went to the clinic to gather supplies to take to the hospital. Brian said it looked as if it had been ransacked by thieves. He suggested that we walk up to the clinic and sort through the mess, and organize and inventory the medications and supplies—just what we had completed minutes before the quake.

By going up there, we would also be able to see and help any villagers in need who were unable to walk down the mountain, across the river, and up the mountain to our yard clinic. Unanimously it was decided to spend our day in this way. Sparvim, a team member and gourmet cook, was going to stay back at the guesthouse and prepare us a meal with whatever she could find in the kitchen. Knowing Sparvim's amazing culinary skills, my previously waning interest in food started to reassert itself, and I was certain that my appetite would find its way back to my stomach by dinnertime.

We had a pleasant walk to the village clinic. It felt good to actually move around; to smile, wave, and greet friends while walking on our familiar route was energizing rather than exhausting. It almost felt normal, in an eerie way. People came to meet and greet us outside the clinic, and the black cloud of Katia's death and the distress of the country seemed to lift briefly as we engaged and connected with our Haitian friends. We did as Brian suggested, taking the whole day to put the clinic back in order. We saw a few villagers who had minor problems, but spent the majority of our time organizing, counting, and chatting and playing with the kids outside the clinic. School was closed and many kids came to see what we were doing back at the clinic. We remembered patients who had touched and moved our souls earlier in the week, wondering where they were and if they were safe and well.

Stacey and a few others drew a mural on the clinic wall with the markers we typically use in the pharmacy. "Today we saw the face of

God," dated January 12, 2010. Reminiscent of the sermon we heard the Sunday before we left for Haiti, when our pastor challenged the congregation to look for the face of God in what we do and see, the wall mural symbolized the souls we saw as we looked into eyes and touched blood and skin on that fateful day, and thereafter. We walked back to the guesthouse together, arm in arm, hands holding little Haitians' hands, forever united by the largest split in recent history.

23 | Decisions

> *The more a man knows,*
> *the more he forgives.*
> —Catherine the Great

WE RETURNED TO THE GUESTHOUSE FEELING REFRESHED AND SMELLING THE AROMA OF SPARVIM'S DIVINE COOKING WAFTING FROM THE WINDOWS, TRAVELING THROUGH THE YARD, AND GREETING US AT THE GATE. THERE WAS ALSO A GROUP OF PEOPLE WAITING FOR US AT THE GATE, STANDING NEXT TO A WOMAN WHO WAS LYING ON HER BACK ON THE GROUND, COVERED WITH A BLANKET AND HER HEAD RESTING ON A PILLOW. A FEW MEN AND ANOTHER WOMAN HAD WALKED SEVERAL MILES FROM PÉTIONVILLE, CARRYING THE SICK WOMAN PROSTRATE ON AN OLD DOOR.

WE WERE GETTING USED TO THESE TYPES OF PROCESSIONALS. I SPOKE TO THE GROUP IN BROKEN CREOLE, AND ONE OF THE MEN COUCHED HIS PART OF THE CONVERSATION IN BROKEN ENGLISH.

Together our communication was comical but adequate. I gathered that the injured woman could not move her legs, that she was experiencing excruciating back pain, and that she had not passed water for more than 24 hours. I invited them into the yard so we could examine the woman. She was moaning, but awake and alert. She had a head injury that would need some suturing, but it didn't seem major, especially compared to the other injuries we had been repairing. After a very careful but complete examination of the woman, we could find no neurological deficits, and no crushing back or neck injuries. We were uncertain as to why she would be experiencing all of these symptoms, although we did feel an amazingly full bladder and a very tense abdomen. She definitely resisted repositioning. She was flat on her back, and she was not going to move.

My wise friend Dawn recalled that she had once had a child in her clinic at home who could not urinate for more than a day and was in similar distress. In her outpatient clinic, they placed the child in a basin of warm water, and the child quickly urinated after just a few minutes of relaxing in the portable bath. We decided to try the same intervention with our ailing woman. Brian and Ray fetched a large kivet filled with warm water from the bathroom. For the sake of the woman's privacy, we asked the men to move toward the front of the yard and turn their backs on the woman. As sunlight was fading, we formed a human wall around her facing outward. With many supporting hands and significant effort, we maneuvered the woman's bottom into the small plastic tub, supporting her back and moving her legs gently as she submerged her perineum and attempted to soothe herself in the warm water. After only a few short minutes and in complete disbelief, she relieved herself, with her warm urine easily mixing with the warm water. Surprise and then relief crossed her face. We couldn't help clapping. The men saw our smiling faces, our thumbs up and all of us exclaiming "*Dacore! Peepee!! Dacore!!! Peepee!!!!*"

Returning our overstated jubilation with smiles, pats on each other's backs, and upturned thumbs, you would have thought we had delivered a baby! For the suffering woman, the past 24 hours probably felt like a long labor. We were all so happy to have done so little, but to have made such a big difference. After a few minutes, she was able to stand. She was shaky but fine. The happy group helped her reposition herself on the portable wooden bed, carried her out of the yard, and aimed itself down the mountain to go back to Pétionville, in the dark.

We went inside for the spectacular meal Sparvim had created, nurturing us with her love and culinary delights, complete with a chocolate cake! We were celebrating Sharon's birthday, we were helping people, and we were alive and unharmed. We could hold our breath for a minute and recognize the blessings in these things. Soon enough, we would be faced with some tough decisions.

The reports of scarce food and water, mini-pockets of rioting, dead bodies everywhere, and pure anxiety were more than our loved ones at home could endure. Many people in the United States were extremely worried about our continued well-being. While we were gone for the day, evacuation options were being placed on the table, both stateside and mountainside. Many coordinated efforts were being considered to expedite our safe return, as soon as possible.

Willem went into Port-au-Prince again and this time made it all the way to the airport and the U.S. Embassy. Could we receive an emergency evacuation through our travel insurance out of Toussaint L'Ouverture International Airport in Port-au-Prince once it became functional? If not out of this airport in Port-au-Prince, was there a way to take a bus to the Dominican Republic and then find an evacuation flight to the States from there? When were the commercial flights planned to resume?

We heard that Préval had requested the United States Air Force to secure the airport, to set up a workable air traffic system, and to temporarily control both the air and the ground at the airport. Specialized troops were in Haiti within 24 hours with generators and a solution for a temporary system to control the emergency air traffic. Coordination was difficult, but the airport was functioning. In fact, the airport, which typically utilized only a few runways, was attempting to service 40 airfields. Planes were filled to capacity with emergency relief workers; search-and-rescue teams and urgent emergency supplies from nations all over the world were landing. A team from Iceland was the first, besides the U.S. forces, to arrive by air on Haitian ground.

The Dominican Republic, being a border country (and not always the most congenial of neighbors) provided almost immediate aid. They sent water, food, and heavy-lifting machinery. Hospitals in the Dominican Republic were made available, and the airport opened to receive aid to be distributed to Haiti. The Dominican emergency team assisted more than 2,000 injured people, while the Dominican Institute of Telecommunications (Indotel) helped with the restoration of some telephone services. The Dominican Red Cross coordinated early medical relief in conjunction with the International Red Cross. The government sent 8 mobile medical units, along with 36 doctors (orthopedic specialists, trauma specialists, anesthesiologists, and surgeons). In addition, 39 trucks carrying canned food were dispatched, along with 10 mobile kitchens and 110 cooks capable of producing 100,000 meals per day. This generous support from the Dominicans may not have been in the media forefront, but it was almost immediate and it was a huge humanitarian effort.

It was Thursday night, January 14, 48 hours after the earthquake. There were no decisions to be made because at that time we still had no options. Air traffic was just starting to enter Toussaint L'Ouverture International Airport in Port-au-Prince, and it was limited to medical teams, search-and-rescue teams, and emergency supplies. The empty planes had started to transfer the injured and walking wounded out of the country for care. As we were able-bodied, we were not yet called to leave the country. A generous company had offered to send a private jet for our retrieval, but could not gain air clearance at the airport, even with a full cargo of supplies. The option of taking a bus to the Dominican Republic, after further scrutiny, did not seem safe or wise; we knew that there were fuel shortages and a huge influx of injured

Haitians at the border. We heard rumors that the commercial airlines were very uncertain as to when they would resume flights. In spite of days of best efforts from home, we still had no options to weigh.

The only decision we made was that in the morning, we would set up clinics at the crossroads of the two main roads in the mountain while Willem, Brian, David, and Ray went to the U.S. Embassy. We felt good, at least, about choosing that course of action.

24 | FRIDAY, JANUARY 15, 2010

> *When one door closes another opens. But often we look so long [and] so regretfully upon the closed door that we fail to see the one that has opened for us.*
> —HELEN KELLER

EACH MORNING WE AWOKE IN HAITI WAS ANOTHER START TO A NEW DAY. ISN'T THAT TYPICALLY THE BEAUTY OF A NEW MORNING: A FRESH START AND A NEW BEGINNING? BUT WHEN THE TRAGEDY OF DAY BLENDS INTO THE SORROW OF NIGHT AND THEN MORNING COMES SO SOON, AGAIN BRINGING MORE TRAGEDY, IT IS DIFFICULT TO BEAR THOUGHTS OF THE NIGHT BEING HOURS AWAY AND FILLED WITH SORROW. THE RISING AND SETTING OF THE SUN, MOON, AND STARS CAN BE TOO FAST AND TOO SLOW SIMULTANEOUSLY. NO MATTER WHAT THE LOCATION, A DAY EQUALS THE SAME 24 HOURS IN ILLINOIS, MICHIGAN, CALIFORNIA, OR HAITI—YET IT CAN FEEL SO DIFFERENT TO EACH PERSON AT ANY GIVEN MOMENT. THE REPETITIVE CYCLE CAN BECOME TOO DRAINING TO REPEAT. TIME CAN TRANSCEND INTO a burden too heavy to bear. It is what it is. There are no earthly reins to halt or accelerate the pattern from day to night to day again, and so it goes. After death we continue on into timelessness and grace under the reign of an eternal peace. Time can be a gift and a blessing, but I have also experienced the nasty trickery of time once before. I know how the Haitian mother feels right now. I also look forward to Heaven.

We woke early Friday morning, ready for a light breakfast and eager to take our traveling clinic on the road. We kept our bags packed and our personal items ready for light travel so that at any given time we could be ready for an unexpected departure. The men were changing into suitable clothes to go to the U.S. Embassy; we were deciding how we were going to organize the supplies.

Willem briefed us on his latest venture into the city. There was a passable route to the airport. When he was at the airport, he heard talk that eventually the emergency planes coming into the airport, once they were unburdened of their cargo, would then be filled with foreigners, for evacuation out of Haiti. We knew of an American who had gone to the U.S. Embassy, and was eventually placed on an evacuation plane after being at the embassy for 36 hours, and was flown to Miami. Willem and Brian thought checking in at the embassy might be worthwhile.

The men were ready to leave, taking with them a list of our names and the passports for everyone on the team. The rest of us were discussing the plans for the day. The satellite phone rang. Mary's husband was on the other end of the receiver, explaining that the stateside group had secured 19 seats on a private evacuation plane. He relayed the tail number so that the team could make the connection once they got to the airport, and made it clear that the passengers would need to be waiting for the plane at the airport in two hours. Willem was willing to take the 19 to the airport, and then check the situation and protocol at the embassy for the remaining four (Annette, David, Brian, and me). Within minutes, our plans for the day completely changed. Readied bags were grabbed, brief hugs were shared, and then Willem with the 19 were on their way to the airport in the back of two pickup trucks. Annette, David, Brian, and I were left looking at each other, wondering what was next.

For the first time since the earthquake, there was traffic on the road down the mountain into the city. Willem understood the urgency of time and took an alternate route: an off-road route on typically untraveled terrain, down the steep mountainside. I was not on this particular truck ride, but suffice it to say that I heard it was as thrilling to some and terrifying to others as any amusement park roller coaster one might pay to experience, with screams uncontrollably belted out throughout the entire length of the ride. There were no safety restraining devices and their wild ride lasted for almost two hours. Once they arrived at the airport, Willem was commanded by the U.S. troops to leave the Americans, not to enter the U.S. citizen area, and to depart quickly from the airport premises. He tried again to accompany them, showing the official his American passport, but was firmly advised that unless he was evacuating, he must exit the grounds immediately. He sadly waved a shortened goodbye and left as he had been sharply directed to do. The 19 were moved into a line with the request that passports be available for inspection. It was hot, it was noisy, it was a whirlwind getting to the airport, but once in the line controlled by the U.S. troops and the U.S. Embassy, there was no chaos. Still, no one knew exactly how the connection with the arranged jet with the known tail number was going to happen.

Finding myself at the computer, I sent an informative email out to let our loved ones know of the hoped-for departure of our 19 compatriots.

Email: January 15, 2010, 9:28 a.m.

From: Sue Walsh
Subject: Coming home

> *Dear family and friends of LBL Haiti team #7,*
> *I just want to give you a quick update. . . .*

There is a plane at the PAP airport through our ASI evacuation insurance that plans to take 19 of our team members out of Haiti to the Dominican Republic. From the DR there are 8 seats available on AA to travel directly to Chicago. The other 11 team members' travel back from the DR to Chicago is insured, but not yet confirmed, so please be patient as we wait for that confirmation. We will let you know more, as we know.

David and Annette Vander Ploeg, Brian and I were unable to travel out of PAP as there were only 19 seats on the evacuation plane available, but rest assured that we are safe and doing fine. We have continued to see injured villagers in the front yard of the missionaries' home, where we are staying. We have a full set of wound care supplies, antibiotics, and pain medication.

Please continue to keep all in Haiti and those traveling in your prayers.

Sue

Brian, David, and Annette stripped sheets from the guesthouse beds, swept the floors, and gathered the used towels. We were basing our plans on the guess that we might be in Haiti for several more days, maybe a week or two. We were uncertain, but we were surprisingly calm and patient. I was contemplating how I might still manage a mini-clinic on the road; being the only remaining medical provider, I was weighing the pros and cons. My mind was wandering around this issue when I saw a new message in my email inbox from the U.S. State Department.

EMAIL: FRIDAY, JANUARY 15, 2010, 11:18 A.M.

From: U.S. Embassy, Port-au-Prince
Subject: Earthquake Recovery Guidance

The U.S. Embassy in Port-au-Prince has issued this message to advise American citizens in Haiti of earthquake recovery guidance in the aftermath of a powerful earthquake that struck Haiti on January 12. An earthquake measuring 7.0 on the Richter scale struck near Port-au-Prince, followed by multiple aftershocks. The U.S. Embassy is working to ascertain the extent of the damage and check on the status of U.S. citizens around the island. The Department of State has ordered nonemergency U.S. government personnel to depart Haiti.

U.S. citizens in Haiti should remain in shelter. If exposed when an aftershock hits, take steps to avoid falling debris by getting to as open a space as possible, away from walls, windows, buildings, and other structures. If indoors, take shelter under a heavy table or desk, or in a doorway. Avoid damaged buildings, and obey all instructions from local authorities. Do not use matches, lighters, candles, or other flame in case of disrupted gas lines. Avoid downed power lines.

Evacuation flights have begun to depart the International Airport in Port-au-Prince. U.S. citizens wishing to depart Haiti should make their way to the airport during early daylight hours, in as safe a manner as possible. They are encouraged to carry their passport and identification, if available, and food, water, and supplies, if possible, as facilities at the airport are limited to nonexistent. If possible, U.S. citizens in Haiti should contact friends and relatives outside of Haiti to inform them of their welfare.

The U.S. Embassy in Port-au-Prince has set up a task force at the Embassy, which is taking calls as conditions permit. The Embassy is working to identify U.S. citizens in Haiti who need urgent assistance and to identify sources of emergency help.

U.S. citizens are urged to contact the Embassy via email at ACSPaP@ state.gov to request assistance. U.S. citizens in Haiti can call the Embassy's Consular Task Force at 509-2229-8942, 509-2229-8089, 509-2229-8322, or 509-2229-8672. The State Department has also created a task force to monitor the emergency. People in the United States or Canada with information or inquiries about U.S. citizens in Haiti may reach the Haiti Task Force at 888-407-4747. Outside of the United States and Canada, call 202-501-4444. For further information and updates, please see the State Department's Consular Affairs website.

The timing of the email from the U.S. Embassy was a little unfortunate. After reading this email, it seemed apparent that it would be

best for us also to go to the airport, register with the State Department, and wait for a flight out of the country. But Willem wasn't here:
He was down at the airport and wouldn't get back to the guesthouse
for hours. By then it would be getting dark, which was not a good
time to be on the road heading down to Port-au-Prince. Cell-phone
connections were still spotty at best, so to catch Willem before he
spent hours at the embassy was a long shot, but we decided to try a
connection from the satellite phone. We would need to ask Willem to
make a rapid turnaround back to the airport—traveling through the
horror again and spending more of his precious fuel. My heart went
out to Willem and his family, witnessing so intimately their country's
destruction and pain.

Brian miraculously reached Willem on his cell phone as he was
on his way to the embassy and explained the informative and direc-
tive email from the State Department. Without hesitation, Willem
confirmed that we should go to the airport and wait for an evacuation
flight. To save time, he would immediately arrange a ride for us from
the guesthouse to meet him halfway down the mountain in Pétionville. He continued speaking in low tones that were hard to hear over
the phone, describing and warning us of the dramatic amount of dust
we would inhale (which was unavoidable), and trying to prepare us
for the acrid smells, the dead bodies, and the utter devastation we
would see. As we gathered our bags, and before we could contemplate
anything on a deeper level, the horn was beeping, the dogs were barking, and our ride was waiting.

The following email came after we had left for the airport.

EMAIL: FRIDAY,
JANUARY 15, 2010, 12:43 P.M.

From: Kevin
Subject: Here is the latest.

The 19 at the airport have safely entered the airport, been processed by the
U.S. State Dept, passed through customs and are now waiting safely. They

are surrounded by U.S. military and feel safe. The plane for them is still on the ground in the Dominican Republic with a news crew waiting to get in. The Haitians are still controlling the airport and they have put on a ground stop for the next 2 hours. Hopefully the airport will reopen this afternoon and the plane can come over and take our people out. We are monitoring the situation as best we can.

We also want to find the best way to get Sue, Brian, David, and Annette back safely. We continue to talk with them occasionally and with each new piece of information we try to make the best plan.

Please continue to pray for everyone.

Kevin

I have previously concluded that my broken heart is my best part. Both my personal and my empathetic pain ignite action, while indifference and complacency make me sluggish. I still had energy, creating a disconnect in my emotions between remaining in Haiti and desiring a swift, safe journey home—I longed to do both.

25 | THE DRIVE

*It is better to light one candle
than to curse the darkness.*
—CHINESE PROVERB

WE WERE PICKED UP FROM THE GUESTHOUSE IN A VEHICLE WITH A FRONT SEAT AND AN OPEN FLAT-BED. THERE WAS ROOM FOR TWO SQUISHED IN THE FRONT WITH THE DRIVER, BUT TWO WOULD HAVE TO STAND IN THE OPEN BACK OF THE TRUCK WITH OUR BAGS. IT WAS NOON, SUNNY AND VERY HOT. WHAT WOULD IT BE LIKE WITH THE HEAT RADIAT-ING FROM ALL OF THE CONCRETE IN THE CITY? WE WERE IMAGINING THE QUALITY AND STENCH OF THE AIR, AND THE EMOTIONS THAT WOULD RISE AS WE SAW THE FALLEN BUILDINGS AND DEAD BODIES. IT WAS NOT POSSIBLE TO CONTEMPLATE THE MAGNI-TUDE OF WHAT WE WERE ABOUT TO EXPERIENCE, BUT THE VISIONS WE FORMED FROM THE MEDIA IMAGES ON TV AND FROM WILLEM'S ACCOUNTS WOULD BECOME REALITIES SOON ENOUGH. BRIAN and David, without question, escorted Annette and me into the cab of the truck, and they hopped into the open bed. It was stifling in the truck. We had to keep the windows open for ventilation and to prevent heat stroke. Brian and David had baseball caps on their heads to help keep them cool, visors shielding their eyes from the sun. We all should have thought to bring bandanas for our noses and mouths.

I knew with absolute certainty, as we started our descent to Port-au-Prince, that the streets, which had become so familiar to me for the last five years, would be forever different. I took some deep breaths of the clean mountain air. I realized that diesel fumes would soon be melding with smells not in my olfactory repertoire. The changes came into view almost immediately as we saw and avoided buckled roads and avalanched walls. Many of the mountain houses we saw during our descent were broken, with structures that were still partially standing looming over matching rubble with eerie shadows. Few people were digging through rocks and bricks of what had been their homes; not many people were on the streets.

As we drove through the destruction and desecration of the smaller city of Pétionville and met Willem in Delmas, we experienced a preview of the full devastation looming ahead. People were digging and crying. The air became gritty and dusty as we traveled through Pétionville and Delmas, even before we reached the streets of Port-au-Prince, stimulating watery eyes, sneezing, and coughing. Brian occasionally took pictures of familiar buildings, where multiple stories had collapsed to the ground, each floor pancaked on top of the next, piled high in a broken layer of three or five or ten, with the rubble from the walls oozing out the sides of the stack. Brian tapped firmly on the roof of the cab to gain our attention and pointed to the side of a large foothill. We looked to the west and saw that where there had previously been thousands and thousands of slum shacks, the mountainside was now barren, and a huge cloud of dust hovered like pollution over the base of the slope. The entire squatter settlement, which had previously covered the whole side of the foothill, had slid down the mountain, crumbling into one gigantic pile of brokenness and death. Thousands and thousands of lives were lost. All of this was too much to process. I was nauseated and dizzy.

We rounded the mountain, trading the heartbreaking vision of the empty mountainside, and the knowledge that so many of the poorest-of-poor Haitians were helplessly crumpled together in the flash of less than a minute, souls stirred up in rock and rubble, for an aerial view of the city. From this distance, an inconsistent collapse of the structures was evident: major buildings were unrecognizable, having buckled like hot pavement. An adjacent structure might stand solidly, while the one behind or next door was merely a heap of crushed walls and smothered lives. There was a cloud of dust over the entire bowl of the city, which became thicker the farther we descended, and a hovering, persistent, unfamiliar stench not detected in the areas through which we had already traveled.

I would have preferred not to know what it was that we smelled. However, because of the scenes both the media and Willem had reported, describing thousands of decomposing and burning corpses in the streets and in mass graves, my keen olfactory sense identified the unfamiliar odor immediately. Before I could consciously halt the process, the putrid scents were stored in my memory bank. There were people in the streets, milling and moving here and there, but not with the familiar energetic buzz of a typical Haitian afternoon. For mile upon mile, there were no merchants or vendors, nothing colorful or lovely; only a picture of urgency and rescue from destruction, on a canvas that was bleak and gray. Brian and David were both coughing in the open bed of the truck, lifting their t-shirts to cover their noses. In the cab of the truck, we rolled up the windows, which caused the already stifling air to become hotter and even more difficult to inhale. We passed by a big white dump truck, not knowing if it was coming or going, and wondering whether it was full or returning for another load. Hot acid burned my esophagus again as I realized what cargo the big white trucks were hauling. Shortly thereafter, we wiped our faces clean with the sleeves of our shirts, using the blend of moisture and salt from sweat beading and tears falling indistinguishably down our filthy faces.

26 | THE TARMAC

Happiness does not depend on outward things, but on the way we see them.
—LEO TOLSTOY

IT WAS NOISY NEAR THE AIRPORT. THE ROAR AND VIBRATIONS OF THE MULTIPLE LARGE AIRCRAFT ON THE FIELD, BEHIND THE DAMAGED AIRPORT OFFICES AND TERMINALS, WERE ALREADY DEAFENING, AS WILLEM PULLED UP AS CLOSE TO THE AIRPORT ENTRANCE AS POSSIBLE. WILLEM PREPARED HIMSELF FOR A SECOND ROUND OF THE OFFENSIVE DRILL HE HAD BEEN PUT THROUGH BY THE AIRPORT OFFICIAL EARLIER IN THE DAY, AS HE PLANNED TO ESCORT US TO THE EVACUATION AREA. WE HUGGED 100 FEET FROM THE ROPES DESIGNATING THE AREA FOR U.S. CITIZENS, AND REASSURED HIM THAT WE WOULD BE FINE, LEAVING HIM STANDING A CONSIDERABLE DISTANCE FROM THE PREVIOUSLY INSULTING U.S. EMBASSY ADMINISTRATOR, WHO WAS CLOTHED IN CRUMPLED SUIT TROUSERS AND A wrinkled white collared shirt, both of which were stained with sweat. We promised that we would speak with Willem soon, calling him with our progress and safety, thanking him for all he had done for us, and emphasizing that we would pray for him and his country. Directives were shouted out by armed troops, as they waved with their machine guns to each designated area, setting a serious and official tone. My head was echoing sounds from the drive and the tarmac even as my heart was reverberating with sounds of my overwhelmed soul.

Snaking along in a line for several hours, on the concrete, baking in the sun, showing our passports as requested, we learned that American planes, along with planes from other countries, had been landing and delivering supplies, troops, and rescue workers for the past 24 hours. The jets were unable to turn their engines off; the airport's restarting generators had been damaged in the quake and were unusable. Refueling was also limited. The walking wounded were triaged and brought to the emptied aircraft for first-priority evacuation. It was estimated that within 24 to 36 hours, those whose homeland was not Haiti and who were not wounded would also be evacuated. We passed several hours outside the entrance of the airport building, within the ropes specifically outlined for American citizens, before we were eventually funneled in and through the crippled building and out onto the tarmac. By then it was about three in the afternoon. David received a text from our team that they had been on the tarmac for a while but they were getting ready to board a plane and make their way back to the States. Separation from the rest of our team had been difficult, but assurance of their safety was all that mattered.

Helicopters were hovering up and down over the city and dramatically landing and taking off from an open, weedy area of the expanding perimeter of the newly viable airfield. The rapidly circulating air created giant swirls of dust, dirt, and dried vegetation, developing back-blasts like that of a tornado, and raining dried particles of all sorts onto our heads, into our eyes, and onto our lips. The amplification of the noise became truly deafening, as the four of us and approximately a hundred other people with American passports were escorted to a designated spot, directly on the tarmac, not more than 100 feet from a row of at least a dozen idling jets. We saw the airport officials' lips moving and arms playing charades to get us into formed queues, but the roar of the engines overwhelmed every voice that was more than a few feet away. We did the best we could to follow instructions: "Stay in a straight line! Do NOT get out of line! Stay in line!" Arms outstretched and facing toward us in parallel fashion, firmly and repeatedly moving up and down, with fingers together and thumbs pointing skyward, like a stiff and stifled cheerleader, they tried to get us in tow.

Brian and David were intrigued by the scene, noting the various aircraft on the runway and the countries they represented. Israel landed a very large modern jet, along with aircraft, jets, and prop planes from the U.S. Air Force, Canada, and many other countries that had been granted airspace and landing privileges. Hour after hour, we watched scores of troops and medics, along with several packs of sniffing rescue dogs, exit the planes and then depart the airfields, passing closely by us in cadence or standing stoically in open-bed trucks, disappearing around the airport building and out into the city.

Crates of supplies were awkwardly unloaded via large-tired forked front-end loaders, which are usually used for material handling rather than cargo maneuvering. Brian became very frustrated watching the process. He knew that if an actual forklift had been available, the driver would have had the necessary maneuverability and precision, using hand levers, to shift and adjust the lifting arms both up and down and back and forth, to easily transfer the cargo. Instead, the front loaders had arms with joints that limited transition to vertical movement, requiring the body of the truck to inch tediously around on the ground to create a useful arm position nearest to the cargo for accurate unloading. The difference between these two working vehicles may sound like minutia, but the time-wasting element of this unloading process was part of the bottleneck on the tarmac. The fact that there were very few trucks large enough to receive the cargo and transport it rapidly and efficiently off the airfield, and out of the airport, also contributed significantly to the stalling and congestion.

At one point, we were distracted by Katie Couric—a brave journalist to come to Haiti at this time—and a small crew lingering near our line. Dusk melded into dark. It was getting late. We barely felt the pangs of thirst and hunger. The fetid jet fumes blending with the pungent air coated our nostrils and throats, creating a rancid taste that would not go away, in spite of constant gum-chewing. We were out of water, which was OK because bathrooms were unavailable. The airport facilities had been significantly damaged. Cracked walls were obvious from the outside of the building, with flooding inside the building also apparent. Evidently water pipes had burst with the severe jostling of the ground during the earthquake.

Groups of evacuees, ranging from 100 to 150 adults, children, and a few babies, were leaving the tarmac together, guided by officials, as either a cargo plane or FEMA (Federal Emergency Management Agency) jet was unloaded and became available. The aircraft carrying evacuees and traveling to the United States had to refuel at various locations, such as Miami, Fort Lauderdale, and Atlanta, and either unload there or continue to another accepting airport or military air base. Our group of 150 was called up around 1:00 A.M., as a large Air Force cargo plane was emptied and made ready to accept passengers. After checking our passports, we were escorted by our line guards onto the runways, walking briskly past at least 10 large planes, and finally arrived at the huge C-137 at the end of the airfield that had been designated as our flight home. We had only our backpacks and small carry-on bags with us, but the evacuating Haitians had the largest pieces of luggage they could find, bursting with important items, as they tried to compact their lives into a suitcase. Brian assisted a struggling older woman with an overstuffed duffel, and commented later that her bag had to have weighed at least 100 pounds. The large entrance ramp, as wide as two trucks with an opening as high as a helicopter, was open for boarding when we approached the plane.

All the passengers waited courteously for one another to walk up the broad plank, claim a spot for their belongings, and finally settle into a seat. Even the tethered jump seats felt luxurious to us, after standing or sitting on hot concrete for the past 12 or more hours. The Air Force personnel checked our passports one last time. Brian and David noticed Katie Couric, in a friendly stance, chatting with someone toward the front and side of the plane. Sitting near her was news anchor Brian Williams, leaning forward, with elbows on knees and cradling his chin in his hands, exhibiting a furrowed brow and looking exhausted. Next to Brian Williams was fellow news reporter Ann Curry, with a contemplative expression. Despite all she had witnessed, she looked fresh and stunning. Annette and David, Brian and I sat together, mirroring Brian Williams's posture and countenance. Passengers dutifully passed along the earplugs given and recommended by the Air Force stewards. We also each received a bottle of water and a granola bar. The pilot informed us that we would need to refuel in South Carolina, and that our passports would be checked again at that point, with our final destination being McGuire Air Force Base in New Hanover, New Jersey. While the pilot was waiting for air clearance, passengers were allowed to use the bathrooms on the plane. We all drank the water and ate the snack.

We sat back, waiting to see what was next. It was extremely interesting to be inside a large Air Force cargo plane. The ceiling of the plane appeared to be at least two stories high, and the jump seats were removable to accommodate large, wide, tall loads. Planked within the floor were long, wide metal strips, with large metal eye bolts inset within the metal planks at even intervals. Hanging every few feet from the walls were wide, thick straps with huge hooked clasps, which appeared to be the correct size to fit precisely into the eyes of the bolts on the floor, securing whatever large cargo, helicopter, truck, or other machine was to be transported. My typical innate curiosity, which had the potential to be annoying to others, was squelched and kept quiet by fatigue, so I didn't assimilate much more. Sitting somewhat stupefied for a long while felt fine, without really caring when we took off. I had stopped clock-watching hours ago. I think I dozed. In an extremely friendly and informative manner, the pilot eventually spoke to us again, preparing us for takeoff.

The sounds radiating from numerous idling jets on the airfield, intermittently revving their engines for taxi and then takeoff, were nothing compared to the roar of the accelerating engines experienced when sitting inside a huge Air Force cargo plane. There was no dozing at this moment! Everyone opened the small boxes containing their newly acquired earplugs and hurriedly inserted the plugs into their ears. No one was in a conversational mood anyway, so it didn't matter that hearing was impossible. Taxiing the aircraft was slow, considering the congestion of the airfield. Our seat belts were on, and we were finally in position for takeoff. The engines were in full throttle and within seconds we exploded into the air with a force that caused all cheeks to waver. It was thrilling if you like airplane takeoffs, but excruciating if you have a fear of flying. We flew rapidly into the dark night sky, leaving an island of misery behind.

My conflicting emotions at that moment were too much to take. I closed my eyes and forced myself to shut down my thoughts and still my mind. I fell asleep until the chill of the circulating air demanded that I don a hooded sweatshirt and blanket. I woke for the second time as we descended into South Carolina.

27 | HOME

*Wherever we look upon this earth,
the opportunities take shape within
the problems.*
—NELSON A. ROCKEFELLER

IT WAS THE MIDDLE OF THE NIGHT IN SOUTH CARO-
LINA WHEN WE ARRIVED TO REFUEL. IT WARMED UP
A BIT IN THE PLANE WHILE WE WERE BACK ON THE
WARM GROUND. MY EARS WERE RINGING, POPPING
AND NEEDING TO BE CLEARED FROM THE VACILLAT-
ING PRESSURE CHANGES IN THE LARGE CARGO CABIN;
IT WAS SIMILAR TO THE EAR SENSATIONS I HAD
EXPERIENCED FOLLOWING MY CHECKOUT DIVE FOR
SCUBA DIVING CERTIFICATION WHEN I WAS IN COL-
LEGE. A CUSTOMS OFFICIAL CIRCULATED THROUGH
THE PLANE, CHECKING PASSPORTS AGAIN NOW THAT
WE WERE ON AMERICAN SOIL.

A FEW OF THE REPORTERS AND PHOTOGRAPHERS
TRAVELING WITH US TRIED TO GAIN CLEARANCE TO
TERMINATE FURTHER AIR TRAVEL AT THIS JUNCTURE,
WHICH WAS NOT ORIGINALLY SCHEDULED; THIS STOP

was supposed to be for refueling purposes only. The customs official had to be re-summoned to process the passengers' requests to depart the plane, which took more than an hour beyond the time allocated for refueling. In normal situations, the other travelers anchored in their seats might have felt a certain level of impatience at someone else's not-in-the-plan requests, but not there and not then. All passengers were docile, apparently grateful to be cared for and brought back to America safely, no matter how long it took. This refreshing attitude, which had been pervasive throughout the previous long day, persisted in the middle of the night and carried through all the following day.

Those of us who enjoyed the thrill of the first ascension in the rapid-fire cargo jet were elated to take off again. Those who were squeamish about the accelerated surge into the air just endured. A few short hours later, in the light of the early morning, we landed at McGuire Air Force Base in New Hanover, New Jersey, once again overchilled from the cool cabin conditions in the upper atmosphere. Shuttle buses were waiting for us when we exited the plane, and were a welcome greeting as tired and saddened Haitians struggled, carrying their heavy baggage, bearing both physical and emotional burdens. It required a number of buses to transport the 150 passengers to the Air Force base headquarters.

We were dropped off directly at the entrance of the large base fitness facility, heartily greeted by uniformed troops who politely held the doors open with one hand. With the other hand, palm open and extended in a friendly way, arm moving in smooth half circles, they gently directed us into the building and down the halls, as if we were dignitaries arriving for an important international engagement. We were assisted to sign in and each received a wristband with our official evacuee number, to be worn throughout the transfer process. First we were funneled into a small room for a brief orientation in both English and Creole; next into a larger room where we placed all of our personal belongings and luggage along a wall for custom officials and their sniff dogs to inspect and approve. Lastly, we were directed into a large gymnasium, where we were offered sandwiches, fruit, snacks, drinks, showers, clean clothes, and a cot to rest or sleep on. Counselors were immediately accessible to aid all evacuees in procuring contact with a known American and assist in making subsequent travel plans, or, for any traveler who had no familiarity with our country or anyone living in the United States, in utilizing available social services. Many Haitians with valid U.S. passports had not been to the country in decades, and ended up being somewhat stranded.

Free phone service and shuttle bus service to a number of civilian airports and train or bus terminals were also easily accessible to all. As we were sorting through our options for returning to Chicago, David received an incoming call from the other 19 on our team. They were split up in Miami, but at that point were all headed back to Chicago, safe and sound, anxiously awaiting contact from us. David amusingly reported that he was "just finishing the best bologna sandwich he had ever tasted!" and that we were checking into flight options for our return back to Chicago. Many personal prayers were answered.

An observer might not have been able to distinguish the differences between our relief to have survived the earthquake and be on American soil, and the Haitians' relief to have survived the earthquake and be on American soil. The differences might not have been evident in facial expression, body language, or verbal exchange as we first entered the evacuation process. However, by that evening we were reunited with our families and friends, lavishing in a lengthy, refreshing shower of any temperature desired, consuming whatever food and drink we desired, and eventually finding comfort in clean linen and our own beds. In contrast, the newly displaced Haitians, both in America and in Haiti, needed to make contact with family or friends, if they had any in this country, or in other areas of Haiti, for an unplanned reunion. They also needed to find the means of traveling to that distant location, and would more than likely spend several more days, nights, weeks, or even months traveling to their destinations. We would have counselors waiting for us to debrief our conscious and unconscious psyches, guiding us through our journey of emotional recovery. The disrupted Haitians had an unplanned journey, in addition to their typically unpredictable life journeys in Haiti, being abruptly split apart from loved ones either by lack of passport or death; they survived it by their strength, resilience, and grace rather than the expertise of professionals. We experienced a life-changing event, together with the Haitian community, on January 12, 2010, and the subsequent hours and days, but we went home to the familiar, with the love and comfort of our lives around us. Every Haitian experienced a permanent life alteration on the same January 12. They were jarred from the love and comfort of their homes and country as they had known it; many suffered through the agony of injury, and all developed a new, chronic sorrow from these catastrophic losses.

We shared an historic event, but even though we were in the same place at the same time, our stories are not the same. This is an imposing, lingering juxtaposition, for the 23 of us who were in Haiti together.

Epilogue: Strength of Haiti, Hope for Haiti

Go back a little to leap further.
—John Clarke

Haiti is a country of strong manual laborers, both in the farming and urban elements. In addition to the tedious task of clearing and planting fields by hand, buildings are also erected inch-by-inch using only hand tools. Heavy machinery is limited and requires fuel and a skilled driver, both of which are in scarce supply. When a man or woman is working, every sinewy muscle is enlisted, and functions synchronously with the mind, adjacent tendons, ligaments, bones, and the workers to the left and the right.

To create a structure, they must first clear the ground of large and irregular rock. Men dig and remove embedded boulders and stone, using picks, shovels, and fingers, most often without gloves. The hand-sculpted ground eventually becomes the flattened form for the foundation. This first step of developing the area for the foundation can take months, and is often done while other workers are crushing rock with sledgehammers to be formed into block bricks. The bricks are then stacked vertically and glued together with mortar, which creates a seemingly sturdy wall and the illusion of a solid structure. To construct a larger building, strong metal rebar, either meshed or stranded, must be located, purchased, and used to support floors, walls, and ceilings, to stabilize the brick blocks and concrete mortar. The bricks are hollow, allowing the rebar to be woven through the bricks and creating a receptacle into which the cement can be poured. Cement is mixed by hand either in ground pits or via a small crank mixer, or both. A human assembly line is created: Buckets are filled with stone, sand, or cement, passed along the line, and dumped with the accuracy and perfect cadence of a group of West Point cadets in a parade.

No uniforms can be seen in this hard-working brigade, only worn garments that will soak up sweat and protect from the blazing sun. There are no supportive or protective boots; only a few workers have knee-high foot coverings made from large, discarded car-tire inner tubes, cleverly rope-tied at the toe and criss-crossed up and around the inserted foot and leg, to provide protection from the abrasive chemicals in the cement. Most workers are either in minimally protective footwear or are bare-footed. Encouraging, rhythmic songs rise up from the laborers who have the freedom to choose to work, as they want and when they want. Slave chants were stifled more than 200 years ago when Haiti became a free democracy.

There is dignity in hard labor. When in Haiti, Brian and I have had the privilege to observe each of the phases of construction, from land clearing, rock crushing, and brick building to foundation pouring and wall and ceiling formation. We have watched welders craft metal into artful window coverings and masons smooth concrete into lovely designs. While noting the justifiable pride of each worker, we have been in awe of the creativity, ingenuity, tenacity, and time required to create even a simple building. Each structure that collapsed in Haiti brought down not just the home equity of property, brick and mortar, but also the human equity of blood, sweat, and tears.

The devastation from this earthquake has stunned and jostled many of us to our knees, both in prayer for the country of Haiti and in our own gratitude, as we once again realize the inequity of lives across the globe. As we returned to Haiti in June 2010, a barrage of questions from family and friends milled around in my mind and I did not know if answers would become available. For example: "Who is in Haiti helping? Who is living in the tent cities and what is it like living there? What is the current source of food and water? What are the hygiene/sanitation conditions? When will the removal of the rubble be complete? When will life be better? Where is all of the aid money going? Where are all the injured? Why is the rebuilding so slow? Why is the government not doing more? How are the children?"

Because of the layers of complexity each such question poses, I believe that precise, concise answers are elusive at best. The consideration of Haiti's political, social, environmental, and cultural history, along with the depth of loss and challenge of recovery, will affect every aspect of human life. I have not yet integrated all of these important areas of knowledge or gained enough cultural humility to support any definitive statements or answers. However, during lengthy conversations with my friends in Haiti, I have gleaned some insights.

Only about 5 percent of the rubble has been cleared during the first six months post-earthquake. The simple question, "When will the removal of the rubble be complete?" thus led me to hours of discussion and contemplation, as well as reflection and struggle, in an attempt to understand and explain. Many factual, humanitarian, and legal issues affect the answer. Many nongovernmental organizations (NGOs) and nonprofit organizations, relief organizations, governments from around the world, the international private sector, and the Haitian government have had a charitable presence in Haiti, setting up tent cities and other forms of relief. The extent and distribution of such aid is uncertain, complicated, difficult to discern, and controversial. At this time, it is easy to find multiple sources surmising that more than 1 million people live in more than 1,000 tent cities, some of which are well-organized with latrines, cisterns for drinking water and shower stations, along with regular food distributions. Other campsites are makeshift at best, with tarps or old sheets thrown across whatever support is available, marking a small spot of respite for those who have absolutely nothing else.

Because of the squatter "laws" of understanding in Haiti, an area of useable ground can potentially become a location for settlement. Once a family or group of people have moved into or onto a land space, it becomes very difficult to evict them. Landowners may be faced with a humanitarian dilemma if they need to displace those on their property. Because of the scarcity of land, heavy machinery, and supplies in Port-au-Prince, an alarming number of official landowners are purposely not removing rubble from their property with any urgency. Because many lack the resources to initiate construction immediately following land clearance, they are fearful that squatters will take over the flattened, prepared land before they can rebuild; if that occurs, they may permanently lose their land ownership status and rights.

Land acquisition in Haiti might seem unconventional in the Western sense, but over the centuries many claims to and gifts of land have left a large number of legal landowners without official deeds, which can make reacquisition impossible. Illiterate landowners can become victims of dishonest lawyers, loan sharks, or urban bourgeoisie who take advantage of the inability to read land titles or other contracts. Gaps in knowledge can certainly lead to misunderstandings, both in Haiti and abroad.

It can be terribly difficult and confusing to comprehend, synthesize, and reconcile the core need for survival with the vision of "better" (obscured for centuries), along with the myriad obstacles the Haitian people face. It is understandable that there would be a plethora of behaviors that an outsider does not and cannot grasp. Taking advantage of a situation that is in front of a person can be viewed in a number of ways, depending on one's cultural lens: Entrepreneurial. Impulsive. Corrupt. Brilliant. Resilient.

As just one example, random tent occupation occurs on sidewalks that closely border streets, have no waste removal or latrine facilities, are overcrowded, and are perfect reservoirs for disease. With internal tent temperatures reaching 140 degrees at midday and threats of entire settlements washing out during the rainy season, living conditions in the tent cities can diplomatically be described as unsafe squalor. In spite of this unpleasant and difficult way of life, some Haitians have purposefully chosen to live in a tent and rent out their intact homes for income.

Another driving force that causes many Haitians to be reticent about returning to living in a solid structure is posttraumatic stress. The ground continues to move with aftershocks, maintaining and escalating anxiety, apprehension, insecurity, and fear. I have observed a similar, though less acute, response that many Haitians have to rain. Willem readily admits that Haitians are scared of and hate the rain. It has caused so much death and destruction for them, no wonder it elicits strong emotion.

Others have been displaced despite the fact that their homes stayed erect. Often their privacy walls and their neighbors' dwellings were damaged or made uninhabitable. Squatters have encroached on much of the flat land that is available, creating unsafe situations and engendering awkward feelings in those who live within the unharmed home, amidst the many who have raised tents and other "temporary" shelters. In spite of the necessary humanitarian action of developing organized tent cities, neither Haiti nor the NGOs are able to provide adequate police patrols in these areas, so an increased potential for crime exists—as would occur in any extremely poor society faced with a high-density population and abject-poverty-level living conditions. It is unfortunate but not surprising to learn that many in the tent cities have found living conditions there to be superior to their previous lifestyles; this sad fact has created a subsidiary population that is currently content in the tents.

Observing human nature in such raw conditions brings to mind Abraham Maslow's 1943 paper, *A Theory of Human Motivation*, in which he describes his "Hierarchy of Needs" theory. In summary form, this hierarchy places essential physiological requirements for life at the base of a pyramid: for humans to survive, they must first satisfy these basic needs, such as breathing, eating and drinking, maintaining bodily homeostasis (temperature), and sex. With basic physical needs satisfied, a person is able to move forward to seek satisfaction of other needs: safety, shelter, health, and well-being; then love and belonging, esteem/respect; and eventually self-actualization. All needs on the continuum are connected and closely interrelated, rather than isolated from each other.

Numerous medical organizations and professionals from all over the world urgently responded to the outcry for medical assistance, setting up temporary surgical and medical tent hospitals. First responders, such as our team, worked under conditions similar to those in a MASH unit. As other teams came, with more staff, equipment, and supplies, they were able to provide better care; thus, we appropriately departed. Many continue to travel to Haiti to help. However, help has never been enough in the past, and help will never be the full answer. But isn't this the same dilemma and paradox that pertains to all societies? More is not always better and no matter how much there is, it is assuredly viewed as never enough.

Solidarity with the Haitian people and sustained commitments to strengthening the public sector, especially in the basic social and economic arenas of health, education, water, and housing, were the call of Dr. Paul Farmer, co-founder of Partners in Health, as he testified at a Capitol Hill hearing hosted by the Congressional Black Caucus, "Focus on Haiti: The Road to Recovery—A Six Month Review." He describes what happened to Haiti on January 12 as an "acute-on-chronic" event. The Clinton Bush Haiti Fund, Build Back Better, also plans to work primarily through partnerships and collaborations with other nonprofit and for-profit entities, particularly Haiti's own. In all activities, Build Back Better plans to work with the Interim

Haiti Recovery Commission to ensure consistency with the Haitian Development Plan.

Haiti's progress is complicated in that the concept of rebuilding is inaccurate for its situation. *Rebuilding* implies that initially something was present that was then destroyed. In such a case, the next logical step would be to recreate what was destroyed, by following a similar blueprint or at least a familiar footprint. This case simply does not pertain in Haiti. Haiti's previous lack of adequate infrastructure—in the civil, social, political, medical, educational, and structural arenas—makes a mockery of the ideology of rebuilding; what they need is more on the order of *creation*. Although help can be simplistic to say and even to do, humanitarian acts of the well-meaning can have unpredictable and undesirable outcomes if provided naively. Haiti's turbulent history, from its start as a prosperous colony nicknamed the "Pearl of the Caribbean" to the present, can make envisioning its future depressing. However, despite its struggles with political despotism, widespread illiteracy, and abject poverty, Haiti radiates beauty from its shores, to its mountaintops and from sparkling eyes to warm smiles. Certainly I have no pat answers, and further discussion is definitely beyond my scope of understanding and philosophical capabilities. However, in my constant state of optimism, I like to remember that without change there would be no butterflies.

During our time in the mountain clinic in June 2010, several survivors of the earthquake made their way to us for care. We were able to provide the basics of health care as we usually do, along with much-needed physical therapy because our team had been expanded to include a physical therapist.

Katia's father was first in line. His was a terribly hard story to hear. He told us of an injury to his fingers the day of the quake, which subsequently became infected. To rid himself of the infection, the unimaginable was done: He purposely dipped his hand in boiling water, which scalded the infection away, but also halted all recovery of potentially viable tissue. His hand became gangrenous and had to be amputated. He also had a leg injury, which compromised his

normal gait, creating a limp and severe back pain. Our physical therapist stretched every one of his muscles all week, and taught him to
continue these stretching exercises to eventually eliminate the limp
and subsequent back pain. He also received physical therapy and
directives to keep his remaining arm and stump muscles healing
properly.

We also heard a more encouraging story: The elder in the village,
who had suffered the severe facial injury, stayed in the hospital for
eight days of recovery following her reparative surgery. We witnessed
the miracle of her survival and her smile.

Email: May 28, 2010

Bonjour from Haiti!

*We arrived safely, to an airport that has recovered in spirit and has become
quite functional. A Haitian rendition of a calypso band was a welcome first
sight and sound, after walking down a long, newly rebuilt reception hallway,
built pre-earthquake to keep travelers off the tarmac. In January, prior to
the earthquake, this addition to the airport was what Brian and I first noted.
It greeted us as a sign of the growth and forward movement of Haiti, while
at the same time we missed the celebrity feeling of exiting directly onto the
tarmac . . . but Brian and I knew that now, on the other side of that wall,
was a cracked and damaged building, still not useable, previously filled with
water from broken pipes, rubble from broken walls, and the chaos of a broken
country. To everyone else it was just a walkway to the bus, which then took
us to the "remodeled" hangar being used as the country's customs center. The
friendly and happy music and vision of the Haitian musicians was an effective
anxiolytic, coaxing us into a relaxed frame of mind and reminding us that
Haiti is as resilient as we are all trying to believe.*

*In the customs hangar, the old wood cabinet/desks, which had been
salvaged from the damages of falling walls and exploding pipes, sat in the
middle of a 3-story-high echo chamber of a recycled hangar, providing us
with a familiar feel as we stepped forward with our passports to be stamped
that our purpose for being in Haiti was for "Pleasure." A blunt blur of truth.*

All but one bag found their way to the repaired turnstile; the only missing suitcase was filled with diaper packs and peanut butter . . . nice but not essential. I am hopeful that whoever establishes custody of that bag will disperse the goods for good use.

The truck ride out of the airport and through Port-au-Prince was a dusty kaleidoscope of visions and emotions, darting from one sight to another. The familiar movement of Haitians busying themselves up and down each street was reassuring. However, the disconnect of the vision came as we watched them sidestep and seemingly ignore the massive mounds of rubble in their paths, in their houses, in their lives. Street vendors were everywhere as usual, setting their goods to the side of a mound of crumbled concrete, or arranging the rubble to suit the presentation of their fruits and veggies, their clothes and their artwork, or how and where they planned to sit.

The apparent strength to carry on is abounding. I spied an elderly man on the street, walking with the assistance of a long rubber-handled lever from a broken foosball table; it caught my eye because of the colorful little soccer men hanging sideways, moving up and down, adding décor and amusement to his cane with each step forward. Behind the vendors and the distorted walls of previous dwellings and stores were tents, sheets, tarps, kids, people, dogs, rubble—all blending together in a dusty, diesel-filled blur.

Being in the open-bed trucks with 40 suitcases and 20 white people, we are a sight. Everyone on the street looks intently at us, with a seeking gaze. The traffic was slow, so it was easy to make eye contact with the stares. Each Haitian, young and old, smiled at my searching looks. A woman nodded toward me with a grin, as I knowingly nodded and returned a laugh as I watched her strong hands doing laundry in a plastic bucket, with her busy baby safely and happily standing in an empty bucket next to her, hands reaching and grasping at her mother's load. I was momentarily reassured but permanently humbled. If I allow myself to recognize the reality of what resiliency means to a Haitian . . . .

On our first day of clinic, we were greeted with 250 people waiting patiently for our offerings and for us. We were careful not to be overwhelmed by the numbers in line, taking time to listen, touch, and connect with each person. The amazing consistency of maladies, concerns, and way of life, from pre- to post-earthquake almost has me lulled into thinking that all effects of Jan. 12 are forgotten.

Sue

EMAIL: JUNE 2, 2010

Hi from Haiti

It's 5 A.M. Wed. morning, I LOVE waking to roosters and dogs, to sunrise and green mountains!!! With sky breaking into peeks of blue, and puffs of cotton clouds rolling down off the tops and dips of the hills, there is no rain and there is no line at the clinic—we are happy!!! I have a peaceful heart from these visions.

We've had an incredibly full week; our team has been able to anticipate the needs of the Haitians and has been intuitive of each others' needs as well, both physically and emotionally. As is typical of our trips, we seemed to have everything we needed. The missioners have a skill set that has been unbelievably diversified, compassionately and carefully treating patients with infections, infestations, injuries, worms, high blood pressure, and trying to provide some comfort for the headaches of the anemia and arthritis of a hard life that is literally always uphill. It's been so amazing to see people again and again over the years, to have a familiar Haitian hug, to see health improving in this small oasis at Mountain Top. We've had just enough health packs, just enough medications, just enough blankets, Crocs, peanut butter, laughter, energy . . . . It is more and more evident with each passing trip that we are bringing all of you with us, as you support us, help us pack, and pray for our work. The only thing we seemed to be missing is more time to spend in Haiti! We all leave our shoes here, hoping they will fit someone and bring modest comfort to a pair of tired but not defeated feet.

We have not been able to get through a day here without a little miracle: reasons for joy but also the unstoppable tears of sadness. A 12-year-old boy blinded by cataracts, likely from measles; a man without a hand and without a daughter he lost in the earthquake; a 7-lb 7-month-old . . . I will never, ever have a completely settled mind as long as it is filled with the remembrance of sick children and the blank stares of a child with malnutrition. I will, however, discipline myself to remember that God is in control, and that He reminds us of His love and hope, and that we can be His hands and feet to do something about the happenings of this world.

I want to share a quote with you from Jimmy Valvano, who was the basketball coach for North Carolina State. He gave a speech at the ESPT awards a month before he died of cancer at age 47. His words are moving: "We should do this every day. Number one is laugh, you should laugh every day. Number 2 is think, you should spend some time in thought. Number 3 is you should have your emotions moved to tears, could be happiness or joy. But think about it. If you laugh, you think, and you cry, that's a full day. That's a heck of a day. You do that 7 days a week, you're going to have something special."

Our trip has been special—thank you for being a part of it!

With much love,
Sue and Brian and the rest of
the Little by Little Team

As first responders after the earthquake, we functioned as if we were wearing broken shoes. Our resources—the hospital surroundings, mountains, roads, buildings, airport, and seaport—were extremely compromised; nothing fit and so much was broken. I am used to being a sprinter in my career in the United States, but in Haiti post-earthquake, I could barely keep walking even in my supportive shoes. The people in Haiti are accustomed to ill-fitting or worn-out shoes. They now have even more obstacles to traverse with such shoes, or no shoes at all.

Even before the earthquake, we focused on the basic need for shoes. Without shoes, bare or badly covered feet invite injury or disease. Worms, in the form of tiny ova that survive in dirt, can easily enter the bloodstream through small fissures in the bottom or the sides of feet. The small parasites can then travel through the bloodstream, grow in the lungs, and mature in the intestines to eventually cause a significant pneumonia, intestinal worm infestation, anemia, and malnutrition. We bring suitcases full of shoes to Haiti to distribute at each clinic. In our view, shoes are definitely a form of medication. We see the same pair of shoes on a child trip after trip. The children wear them until the shoes are so worn out that they fall off and are left on the side of the road. Broken shoes are a fixture in Haiti, a symbol representing the varied struggles Haitians go through every day.

It would be amazing if we could put on shoes of empathy and walk the full mile with both our close and our distant neighbors. We initially find it intriguing to try on another's shoes when we see or hear about their different walks of life. Nevertheless, when we attempt to wear their high heels, flip-flops, loafers, or work boots, after a while even the most attractive, casual, or supportive shoes of another person can become uncomfortable. They pinch at the toes, flip too loud, flop off, or get soggy with sweat. Even good footwear can be uncomfortable when you're trying to stay the course. How, then, do we borrow shoes that are dirty, smelly, or broken and go the distance?

Because of our sturdy shoes, we did stay on our feet. Typically we wear good athletic shoes to Haiti in anticipation of giving them away. Our eyes start sizing up feet on the last day of our clinic, trying to find the right fit for someone in need. We wear old shoes or a pair of flip-flops home (which can be pretty chilly in Chicago in January). Giving away our shoes feels like offering up a piece of ourselves, which can hug, support, and bring comfort to the soles of our Haitian friends, as we also remember the souls of each. This is just a little way we can continue to walk with them, even as we leave.

READER DISCUSSION GUIDE

1. At the start of *Walking in Broken Shoes*, the author briefly shares her own personal tragedies, not only that of losing her son, but also of being struck by a car. Why did the author share this personal part of her life? Did memories of your own personal stories come to mind? If so, what emotions did these memories elicit, and how did those memories set the tone for your continued reading? Did this help you relate to the author's stories of Haiti?

2. The author starts each chapter with a quote that holds special meaning for her, to provide the reader with another dimension to the author's own words. Was there a particular quote that resonated deeply with you? Which one, and how did it affect you?

3. "Be still and know that I am God" (Psalm 46:10) is the first quote in the book. Why do you think the author began with that quote? Did she listen? Have you ever been stilled by an unplanned occurrence or possibly a purposefully scheduled event? Were you able to listen? What have you heard? Did you respond?

4. Throughout the book, there are multiple accounts of gut-wrenching situations. The author mentions that her broken heart is her best part. Why does she say this? What does she gain from her broken heart? How does she respond? How do you respond to heart-breaking events in your life?

5. Metaphors and symbolism can help readers understand and identify with an author's point of view.

How did the author thread both into her writing? Did this bring you more deeply into her stories? Did you have a different understanding of the title after you finished reading the book? What does empathy mean to you?

6. Teamwork and the importance of synergy are discussed a number of times, in varying ways, throughout the book. What examples of teamwork did you find in the book? Are there examples of teamwork in your life that you could share?

7. The author tells her stories of Haiti and gives her personal account of being in the earthquake. Her faith journey is also a part of her stories. She attempts to express to readers that she is no one special. Yet, with deep faith and the camaraderie and support of so many, little by little she has done so much. Was there a particular story that resonated more deeply with you than another? Which one and why?

8. Even though the author takes the reader through very specific stories, do you think she is guiding readers to seek out their personal stories and journey? Do you have a story that can be shared with others? What is your personal journey?

9. While reading these stories of Haiti, the reader becomes a witness to inequity, suffering, and injustice. What are examples found in the book? Do you recognize anything similar in your life or in other situations near or far? Is your faith questioned or strengthened? Are you called to act?

10. The author leaves us with hope. Can you identify that hope not only for Haiti but also in yourself and in serving others?

BIBLIOGRAPHY

Girard, Philippe. (2010). *Haiti: The Tumultuous History—From Pearl of the Caribbean to Broken Nation.* New York: Palgrave Macmillan.

Huitt, W. (2007). Maslow's hierarchy of needs. *Educational Psychology Interactive.* Valdosta, GA: Valdosta State University. Available at http://www.edpsycinteractive.org/topics/regsys/maslow.html

Hunt, Linda M. (2001). Beyond cultural competence: Applying humility to clinical settings. *The Park Ridge Center Bulletin,* issue 24 (November/December), pp. 3-4. Available at http://www.parkridgecenter.org/Page1882.html and http://www.parkridgecenter.org/Page1880.html

Kidder, Tracy. (2003). *Mountains beyond Mountains: The Quest of Dr. Paul Farmer, a Man Who Would Cure the World.* New York: Random House.

Louis, André J. (2007). *Voodoo in Haiti: Catholicism, Protestantism and a Model of Effective Ministry in the Context of Voodoo in Haiti.* Mustang, OK: Tate Publishing & Enterprises.

Tervalon, Melanie, & Murray-Garcia, Jann. (1998). Cultural humility versus cultural competence: A critical distinction in defining physician training outcomes in multicultural education. *Journal of Health Care for the Poor and Underserved, 9*(2), 117-125. Available at http://info.kp.org/communitybenefit/assets/pdf/our_work/global/Cultural_Humility_article.pdf

About the Author

SUSAN WALSH

Sue Walsh currently enjoys her work as a primary care pediatric nurse practitioner and as a clinical instructor of graduate nursing students at the University of Illinois in Chicago. Combining her expertise in infant, child, and adolescent health care with her passion for serving vulnerable populations, she and her husband, Brian, have been leading medical mission teams to Haiti since February 2006.

Sue and Brian have been married for more than 30 years, have raised 3 children (Brad, Maggie, and Kyle), and have more than 30 nieces and nephews. The love of family and friends is Sue's greatest blessing, but the ability to be God's hands and feet is Sue's deepest joy.

In May 2003, the horrible tragedy of a motor vehicle accident took the life of Sue's oldest son, Brad. After a short leave of absence Sue returned to work. A few months later, that same year, a car made an illegal turn and struck her as she was crossing a busy intersection walking to her car. She now reflects back on that time as a gift of stillness and rest, as she was forced to break away from her empty daily routine and recoup for several months. That quiet period was faith building and deeply healing of both her broken body and her broken heart. She continues to see great joy in this world.

Sue realizes that we all endure varied forms of tragedy and loss throughout our lives. She knows that our response to such events is very personal and that the collective experience of the 2010 earthquake in Haiti did and will continue to elicit both profound and subtle emotions and actions in many. It is in keeping with these thoughts that Sue hopes to engage her readers in undertaking their own reflections of tragedy, loss, faith, and action.

Little by Little is a nonprofit 501(c)(3) organization, supported by many across the country, that was established by Susan Walsh and the dedication of many volunteers to faithfully partner with those in need of improved health and well-being, specifically in Haiti. Together with a very committed group of individuals, Little by Little continues to pursue its mission, recognizing that the sustainability of this work is paramount to the vulnerable population they serve in Haiti.

Thank you for purchasing this book. A portion of the proceeds from the sale of *Walking in Broken Shoes* will help to support the Walshes' continued medical mission work in Haiti.

To make a direct donation to Little by Little, please visit the website: www.littlebylittlehaiti.org

Mountain Top Ministries

Mountain Top Ministries was founded, and continues to be led, by Willem and Beth Charles. Willem, a natural-born citizen of Haiti, and Beth, a native of Indiana, are dedicated to seeing Mountain Top Ministries reach its goal to serve the people of Haiti and to spread God's word. As a nonprofit 501(c)(3) organization, they are dedicated to assisting the Haitian people by providing Christian education, providing quality medical care, and training Haitian ministers.

Vision Statement
Mountain Top Ministries exists as a resource that ignites a vision in the Haitian people for their country to recognize their true potential, so that they may take spiritual ownership of their nation to defeat generational poverty village by village.

Mission Statement
Share the good news of Jesus Christ with the families in the village of Gramothe and the people of Haiti by providing for their spiritual, physical, and academic needs.

MTMHaiti.com

For more information regarding this book,
please visit

www.walkinginbrokenshoes.com

Readers of this book will also enjoy
Growing Up Yanomamö:
Missionary Adventures in the Amazon Rainforest
Christian Biography Book of the Year
Award Winner!

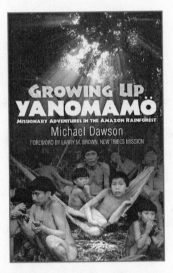

The *New York Times* describes *Growing Up Yanomamö* as
"Huck Finn with an Amazon twist." Michael Dawson recounts
his adventures growing up and working with the last stone-aged
tribe in the world living deep in the Amazon rainforest.

Visit Grace Acres Press at
www.GraceAcresPress.com
for more books to cultivate joy in your life.